Poorly Performing Schools and How To Manage Them

No school can afford to have poorly performing teachers or other staff; they provide a poor education for children and give poor value for money. This book will help headteachers, managers and governors diagnose and tackle poor performance where it has arisen, and prevent poor performance in the future. It offers a structured framework to tackle such problems and identifies a number of potential solutions.

The book investigates a whole range of solutions and issues and includes detailed case studies on: remedial action; disciplinary action; legal and moral issues; employment law; and dismissals and appeals.

Brian Fidler is a Professor at the School Improvement and Leadership Centre at the University of Reading. **Tessa Atton** is a trainer and former acting secondary head.

Poorly Performing Staff In Schools and How To Manage Them

Capability, competence and motivation

Brian Fidler and Tessa Atton

London and New York

First published 1999
by Routledge
11 New Fetter Lane, London EC4P 4EE

Simultaneously published in the USA and Canada
by Routledge
29 West 35th Street, New York, NY 10001

Routledge is an imprint of the Taylor & Francis Group

© 1999 Brian Fidler and Tessa Atton

Typeset in Garamond by Routledge
Printed and bound in Great Britain by
Biddles Ltd, Guildford and King's Lynn

British Library Cataloguing in Publication Data
A catalogue record for this book is available from the British
Library

Library of Congress Cataloging in Publication Data
A catalogue record for this book has been requested

ISBN 0–415–19817–8

Contents

PART III

PART IV

Illustrations

Tables

Flowcharts

Figures

Notes on the authors

Tessa Atton. After an early career as an interpreter and youth worker, a family move prompted her to enlist as a supply teacher. By the end of the year she had a post as Head of Modern Languages, and became Senior Teacher in the same school two years later. Within four years she had become a Deputy Head responsible for curriculum and staff development. She had long periods of Acting Headship, especially during an OFSTED inspection, a change in the age of transfer and an extensive building programme. During this time she was in great demand as a county trainer. She enhanced her management skills by taking an MBA (awarded with distinction) and now teaches management at Henley Management College, Reading University and as a freelance consultant. She is an NPQH trainer.

Graham Clayton. Graham is the Senior Solicitor at the National Union of Teachers and a practising specialist in teacher-related law. He has published regularly on aspects of the subject. He is also the originator of the Law Manager software produced by SIMS and the NUT company Law Matters.

Brian Fidler. Brian is Professor of Education Management at the University of Reading. He trained as a teacher at the College of St Mark and St John, Chelsea, before taking higher degrees in physics at the University of Sheffield. He became a lecturer in physics at the University of Huddersfield before developing an interest in the development of the educational system. After a higher degree in educational policy and planning at the University of Lancaster and a research fellowship at the University of Birmingham, he began teaching school management at Reading in 1981. He is course leader for the MSc Managing School Improvement. The members of this part-time course are all senior staff from schools and it is because of issues raised by members of this group over the years that an interest has developed in the management of poorly performing staff. He has written and edited ten books, including a chapter on poor performers in *Staff Appraisal and Staff Management in*

Schools and Colleges published by Longman in 1992. He is Treasurer of the British Educational Management and Administration Society and editor of the international journal *School Leadership and Management*.

Preface

All of us remember going to school as pupils and can remember, probably in great detail, the effect various teachers had on us. We can remember the inspirational teachers, those who we were afraid of but who we respected, and those who challenged and motivated us. But we can also remember those embarrassing times when we took advantage of a weaker teacher's lack of confidence, knowledge or classroom skills and we look back, probably with some anger or resentment, at those who had failed to prepare us adequately for our examinations. One of us (T.A.) distinctly remembers the disbelief she felt when, as a student, she opened a Latin 'A' level paper to discover that her group had not covered any of the subjects in sufficient detail to be able to achieve good marks. They were a group of able students with A grades in their other subjects but D or E in Latin.

This book has come about as a result of discovering a mutual interest in the subject. One of us (B.F.) had written a theoretical chapter on poor performance in *Staff Appraisal and Staff Management in School and Colleges*, published by Longman in 1992 (Fidler 1992). The other (T.A.) was recently asked to run an LEA course for headteachers on working with any poor performers on their staffs. We both recognised the need for a book to help headteachers and others dealing with staff who were performing poorly. We were both committed to an approach which was firm but fair and concentrated on prevention rather than remedial action.

We decided that a book such as this, if it is to be helpful to senior staff in schools dealing with poor staff performance, should be illustrated with examples of different approaches. We expected that we should have great difficulty in assembling examples but, to our surprise, we found that this was not so. In our experience, it is a myth that poorly performing staff in schools have not been tackled and that it has been impossible to remove staff who could not improve. Nor are the examples here unique. We have already encountered the situation where teachers have read these examples and thought that they recognised a case, when, in fact, it was from a different part of the country.

We have tried to include a full range of actual examples. These, however, over-represent long-standing examples of poor performance, since we believe that these are more difficult to deal with than recently appearing signs of poor performance and that more help is needed in these cases. Thus the picture given here may be overly negative, since we believe that most cases of recently diagnosed poor performance improve and these cases are under-represented here.

We are very grateful to Graham Clayton for writing the legal chapter (Chapter 5) and for emphasising the seriousness of the implications for the poor performer of any actions taken by the school. He found time to write this chapter at relatively short notice and was able to include the implications of the *Draft Code of Practice on LEA–School Relations* as these were known in May 1998 (DfEE 1998).

We are also very grateful to all our many informants who have provided us with the many actual examples of poor performance being tackled. We regret that we cannot thank them here by name because that might break the guarantee of anonymity which we gave to the cases that we have included. In some examples we have changed inessential details of the cases in order further to ensure their anonymity.

Brian Fidler and Tessa Atton, The University of Reading, June 1998

Chapter 1

Introduction

There have always been teachers who, for whatever reason, have not carried out their role to a satisfactory standard. It has long been assumed that schools exist in order to enable pupils to learn and develop to the limit of their potential but it is only fairly recently that this has been articulated in terms of schools' aims and objectives. Once articulated, the next step is to interpret these aims through action: staff training and development, appraisal, evaluation of performance, formal inspection and so on, to the current scene with league tables and target setting. The intention of these procedures is to ensure a consistency of quality educational experience for pupils wherever they are and whatever their ability.

Inconsistency in the quality of staff performance can be the result of a whole range of factors. An unexpectedly poor examination result is not necessarily the direct result of poor teaching. It could be because of resourcing decisions made two or three years previously. It could be pupil grouping arrangements dictated by timetabling constraints. It could be the result of external pressures on either the teacher or the pupil. Once detected, the determination of the reasons for poor staff performance is a complex exercise.

It is the aim of this book to explore what poor performance is and how it can be identified, to look at the range of factors causing performance to drop below the standard required and, most importantly, to look at ways that senior managers, governors and LEAs can and have worked to remediate such problems.

Definition

'Poor performers' is the euphemism which this book uses for those employees who are not performing satisfactorily. 'Poor performers' have major failings in a number of critical aspects of their work. They fall below a threshold of satisfactory performance on a number of criteria: they are not just unsatisfactory in one small aspect of the job.

This introduces the concept of a benchmark which can be used to identify the minimum satisfactory performance. Where this exists, and is generally agreed, then the suspected poor performer can be assessed against the criteria to gauge the extent to which he or she falls short. Where such a benchmark does not exist, even notionally, then such a benchmark needs to be set up so that everyone is aware of the expectations of satisfactory performance. Inevitably, there will be employees performing at a variety of levels of performance. Unless there are clear expectations of performance, some very good but nervous employees will suspect that their performance is in question because they set themselves exacting levels of performance. It is important that such groups are reassured that their levels of performance are not in question.

What is an appropriate benchmark will depend upon the situation. The context of the school and its history will influence what are appropriate benchmarks. Thus it is 'criteria in context' which are important for defining the expectations of a satisfactory teacher or other worker. For a teacher, this is the 'professionally acceptable standard' referred to for teachers in the *Revised Outline Capability Procedure for Teachers* produced in November 1997 (DfEE 1997b). We think this is best laid down at school level. Such a benchmark should lay down standard operating procedures, such as marking and assessment policies, attendance at meetings, required deadlines for paperwork and so on, in addition to more general expectations of teaching competency.

Recency of effect

We have categorised poor performance as either:

a   of long standing, or
b   having just appeared.

In our experience, it is likely that different managers will be taking action in each of these two cases. In case (a) it is likely to be a new manager, while in case (b) it is likely to be an existing manager. Existing managers are most likely to be taking action on poor performance which has only just appeared. It will have come to their notice as being out of the ordinary for this member of staff and they will expect that its causes can be located and a solution found. On the other hand, existing managers are unlikely to have such expectations about long-standing poor performance. They are likely to have become accustomed to this level of performance as the norm, and have come to accept that this is tolerable. They are likely to try to ameliorate and work round such poor performance. They are unlikely to do anything about it unless they are under particular pressure to do so or feel themselves under such pressure. Financial pressures and regular school inspections have provided some new incentives to tackle difficult problems of this type.

We find that it is most likely to be a new manager who comes into a school who notices performance which is out of the ordinary and unacceptable to him or her. He or she is likely to be the one to tackle long-standing poor performance. In many ways this is easier because there are no long-standing relationships, nor is there the need to justify why no action has been taken in the past. A new person also means that it is a fresh and unprejudiced eye which looks at the situation. The new manager will need to collect evidence to ascertain that there really is a problem.

A further situation which has come into existence recently is a combination of the above. Here, an existing manager is dealing with long-standing poor performance, either with the prospect of a school inspection by OFSTED inspectors or after such an inspection. In this case, the manager feels under renewed pressure to tackle a problem which has been neglected. The options are rather greater before inspection than afterwards. However, the option before inspection, of trying to cover up poor performance, may rebound on the school. In the case of one small infants' school, a poor teacher who was also the English co-ordinator was helped to show evidence of satisfactory teaching during the inspection week, but it was the lack of progress in English which was then picked up by the inspection report. This teacher was not able to provide such leadership, and indeed after the inspection her teaching performance also began to decline.

While dealing with poor performance is never easy or pleasant, we have recognised an increasing level of difficulty in the cases identified above, as shown in Table 1.1 below.

Teaching and non-teaching staff

Although a good deal of the book deals with varying kinds of examples of teaching staff who are poor performers, there is also some consideration of other staff in schools who may be poor performers. Although there are separate capability and disciplinary procedures for teachers, generally there are only disciplinary procedures for other employees. It is our contention that each school should have a policy and procedures to deal with poor performance for all staff. There should be the equivalent of capability procedures for non-teaching staff to cover the cases where they do not have a clear understanding of the requirements of their job or do not have appropriate skills.

Table 1.1 Degree of difficulty of dealing with poor performance

Poor performance	Manager	Degree of difficulty
Recent	New or existing	Moderate
Long-standing	New	Considerable
Long-standing	Existing	Immense

Recent changes

This book examines the causes of poor performance and suggests both how to prevent poor performance and how to deal with it. It illustrates these theoretical ideas with a wealth of examples. These are closely based on real examples which have mainly occurred in the 1990s. In some cases, inessential details have been changed to preserve the anonymity of the informants and the characters. Later sections of the book contain more detailed case studies which can be used for discussion purposes. All the examples here need to be analysed for any changes which might be necessary in present circumstances due to:

- revised outline capability procedures introduced in November 1997
- changes to regulations on early retirement
- lower tolerance of poor performance

Following concern at the sometimes protracted timescale which existing procedures took for dealing with poor performance, the *Revised Outline Capability Procedure for Teachers* was agreed by the DfEE and teachers' unions in November 1997 (DfEE 1997b). These provide for accelerated procedures 'in extreme cases where the education of pupils is jeopardised' within four weeks and a normal procedure which should be completed in two terms.

One feature of a number of the examples of solutions to poor performance in the past included in this book is the possibility of early retirement. This has generally meant retirement after the age of 50 but before normal retirement age. In September 1997, the government made changes to the pension regulations which required employers (LEAs and schools) to fund any costs arising from early retirement. Previously, such costs had been borne by the pension fund itself. Such a financial commitment for either LEAs or schools is likely to be prohibitive and so it is generally assumed that early retirements in future are likely to be less frequent. This has severe implications for dealing with poor performance. As many of the examples given here show, although early retirement is not without its problems, it has provided an 'honourable way out' for many poor performers. The implications of the withdrawal of this facility may necessitate alternatives to a number of the examples in this book.

Finally, a further change which has taken place over the last few years is a decreasing tolerance of poor performance by teachers and others. A number of the examples contained here have involved protracted and sometimes intermittent periods of active work dealing with poor performance, often with excessive consideration of any consequences for the poor performer. Many cases which were treated as cases of capability might alternatively have been treated as cases of discipline and brought to a more speedy conclusion. While we hope that the case studies provide a reality to the ideas presented here, we are aware that they are a product of their time and that much useful discussion could result from reconsidering how they might be treated in the different circumstances, which we believe to exist now for the reasons cited above.

Interests of children

Although the climate may have changed, we believe that the essential justification for tackling poor performance has not. The reason we believe that poorly performing staff in schools cannot be ignored is that, directly or indirectly, these staff adversely affect the education of children and young people. Schools exist, first and foremost, to educate children, and that is why teachers and others are employed in schools.

Not only may poor performers directly affect the education of children, but they may also have an indirect effect. Poor performance may prevent other staff from teaching well, in addition to affecting staff morale where other staff can see that they are continually being let down by one or two staff who are not performing satisfactorily.

Few senior staff can approach dealing with poor performance with anything but great trepidation. It is not an enjoyable task. However, many headteachers have been sustained through the process by a conviction that what they are doing is necessary if they are to serve the interests of children, and that they would be letting down the children in their care if they did not take action. As one headteacher put it, 'keep your eye on the children'. She offered this advice both to assess the effects of classroom performance and also as a reminder to ensure that the interests of the children are upheld within the school.

Determination and open-mindedness

This brings us to what we believe to be an essential attitude to the management of poor performers. We are convinced that the only guarantee of ultimate success comes if the prospect is approached with an absolute determination that the poor performance will not be allowed to continue. This means that if all else fails, the poor performer will be dismissed. This may seem unduly pessimistic in view of our experience that most poor performance can be corrected, if it is tackled appropriately and tackled early, but it is an attitude of mind which we believe to be indispensable. This is because it is this conviction which ensures that some progress is made when conditions appear to be at their toughest. The alternative is to make progress when possible and accept defeat when the first obstacles appear.

We believe that this absolute determination is more likely to be in the poor performer's ultimate best interest too. Such determination is likely to lead to a more positive outcome because it is clear that the relentless driving force is spurred on by a need to defend the interests of children and that they cannot be let down. The alternative is for the process to stall when obstacles appear. However, it is our experience that in this case, the same issue will come up again in the future when the problem is more entrenched and the prospects of a positive outcome from the poor performer's point of view are much reduced.

We have produced this book to sustain headteachers and others in tackling poor performers, and also to ensure that they are aware of and follow good ethical practice in dealing with poor performers. We defend neither poor performance nor the unscrupulous hounding of poor performers, or even worse, the indulgence of personal prejudices by headteachers. We believe that the hallmarks of good practice are:

- the assessment of performance based on evidence, not hearsay;
- an approach combining support with a determination to secure acceptable improvement;
- the seeking of innovative solutions, rather than an unbending obduracy which only seeks improved performance in an unchanged job;
- giving consideration to the dignity of the poor performer, and honourable solutions are sought rather than punitive ones;
- learning lessons about the prevention of future poor performance, rather than accepting poor performance as inevitable;
- ensuring the interests of children are paramount.

The structure of the book

The book is written for all who have to deal with poor performers – heads and senior staff in schools, governors and LEA advisors and inspectors. It aims to treat the problem of poor performance in a comprehensive way both as regards the types of staff covered – heads and other teaching staff and also teaching support staff – and also as regards the reasons for poor performance and possible solutions.

Part I begins with a chapter that outlines the ways in which the poor management of staff can contribute to poor performance and makes the case for good staff management as the best preventive measure. It deals with selection, induction, motivation and monitoring, appraisal and development.

Five further chapters follow in this section. The first two present a theoretical framework for analysing and solving problems of poor performance. The next chapter outlines the evolving legal framework within which schools operate employment law. The final two chapters in this section examine the part which the governing body of a school plays, and concludes that it is in identifying and dealing with poorly performing headteachers that governors make their most important contribution.

Part II looks in detail at particular issues – recently discovered poor performance – and at particular groups of staff – temporary problems, new staff, established staff, management positions and teaching support staff. A number of actual examples are presented and their implications analysed.

Part III consists of twelve further detailed case studies. This gives a more full picture of a number of cases of poor performance. These convey the progress of issues over time so that a better understanding of the complexity of the issues can be gained. These case studies are intended to be sufficiently detailed so that they can be discussed by groups of staff. We envisage that small groups of staff who may be dealing with poor performance or who are being prepared to deal with poor performance could discuss these examples and in particular examine how they might be treated differently now when the prospect of early retirement as an option can be expected to be more difficult to obtain, capability procedures are expected to be time limited and whether some of the cases should perhaps have been considered as disciplinary issues rather than capability issues.

Finally, Part IV concludes with a summary of the main points made in the book, and three flowcharts which are intended to provide a framework for action.

This book is intended for practitioners, and so few references are used in the text. There are some suggestions for further reading associated with each chapter if the interested reader wishes to follow up some of the ideas.

Part I

Chapter 2

Managing staff

Introduction

It is our contention that much poor performance of staff results from poor management at some stage in the past. Thus we believe that a major emphasis should be on the prevention of poor performance through good staff management. All the stages of managing staff are potential contributors to poor performance. These stages are:

- selection
- induction
- motivation and monitoring
- appraisal
- development

Approaches to staff management

There are a number of approaches to staff management which can prove successful. Two contrasting approaches are:

- structural
- strong culture

By structural, we mean that there is a clear management structure with formally delegated responsibilities and meaningful job descriptions. How such management responsibilities are discharged is then a matter of management style. With this approach there should be a clear responsibility for identifying and dealing with poor performance, and there should be well-established procedures for providing a clear framework within which to act. Although this may sound a little mechanistic, the practice can be very different depending on the spirit in which such a system is operated. The management style can range from the informal and encouraging to the formal and restrictive. The framework provides the structure to guide operations if things begin to go wrong.

By strong culture, we mean that the organisational objectives and values are articulated and widely shared by the leadership and staff of the organisation. In this way, individuals are empowered to act in ways which are consonant with the culture. Formal structures are weak, and managerial oversight is largely unnecessary because individuals 'know' what the organisation requires them to do. In this kind of organisation, choosing new staff who will fit in with the culture is very important because, without formal structures for support, it is very difficult to deal with poor performers. As many of the cases in this book show, staff who are initially competent do not always remain so and it is therefore unrealistic to assume that poor performance will never be a problem.

In addition to formal management positions, there may be other relationships which may be used to guide the performance of staff. Mentoring is a way of assisting members of staff who take on new tasks and can also be used to provide advice and guidance thereafter. This represents a different kind of relationship compared to a managerial one, where the approach to management is rather formal. Thus some styles of management can incorporate mentoring while others cannot. If incorporation is not appropriate, then separating them and assigning the mentoring role to someone who does not have line management responsibility for the mentee, but who has their trust, is a worthwhile alternative.

Much activity in school takes place in teams and groups. Not all groups are teams, nor do they need to be but, in an integrated activity such as teaching where programmes of study need to be formulated which are progressive as children move through the school, individuals do need to plan and work together in some way. Working in a 'team' is a very close form of working which needs much attention to develop it, and this does not suit everybody. There are dangers in working closely together in groups – groupthink and risky shift are but two of them. Periodically, where there is opportunity, teams should be reformed to prevent these. Working parties can be created to work on specific tasks for limited time periods. This gives the opportunity to bring individuals together who may benefit from such stimulation. It also offers the opportunity to form teams using some of the ideas of Meredith Belbin. Grouping individuals with complementary attributes within a team can make the team more effective and a better problem-solving device. Many formal groups have to be formed on functional grounds, and there is little chance of being able to incorporate these personal requirements. Working parties and task groups do offer such an opportunity and can be highly developmental for individuals by giving them a challenge and bringing them into contact with stimulating colleagues.

Staff selection

Staff selection is perhaps the most crucial stage in staff management, and may often be found to be the most obvious source of poor performance in staff who have only recently been appointed to a school.

Staff selection often begins with a consideration of whether the leaving person needs replacing and, if so, in what form. An exit interview with the departing member of staff should help ascertain the exact nature of the job and the skills and attributes required. After an assessment of the post that needs to be filled and a job description has been formulated, the skills and attributes which are deemed necessary to do the new job need to be analysed. These should be categorised as essential skills and desirable attributes. When these have been determined, an advertisement needs to be drafted and circulated. This needs to be able to communicate the requirements of the job and the culture of the school to potential candidates so that they can judge whether they think they can do the job, and also whether they wish to work in this kind of organisation.

One of the authors of this book (Brian Fidler) has written elsewhere that the selection of staff is a two-stage process. The first stage is to shortlist those who are capable of doing the job. This shortlist will obviously be based on only partial evidence, from application forms, but should indicate those who show every indication from their records as having the skills to perform the job. Any face-to-face contact then has a dual function. On the one hand, it should provide a cross-check of the candidate's ability to perform the job. This may be achieved by a series of interviews with different people in the school, and also a series of simulated tasks to see the candidates in action. Interviews involve candidates answering questions and talking about what they have done, their thoughts and attitudes to the job and what they might do in hypothetical situations. While this only tests an ability to talk about the job, doing this to different groups over an extended period when different aspects are being probed will provide better insights into the thinking of the candidates than a single interview. This evidence, in conjunction with performance on simulated tasks, should provide a great deal of valid evidence about ability to do the job and how the job might be done. From this, the competence of candidates can be assessed.

The second, and equally difficult, task is to select the best fit between the competent candidates and the school. This is not a straight choice of who will fit in best. It all depends on what is wanted in the school. Collecting together like-minded people is very dangerous for the long-term health of an organisation. For one thing, too much similar thinking may induce groupthink with all its attendant disadvantages; secondly, if radical change is required there may be no capacity for new thinking to start or flourish. Thus for any job there may be two choices: someone to fit in or someone to 'stand out'. The person to 'stand out' represents an attempt to change practice within the school. The person to stand out must not stand out too much; otherwise it may be quite painful for all concerned. The person needs appropriate social skills so that they can express contrary opinions without provoking too much dissension. He or she will also need appropriate support (see the example of Rob in Chapter 8).

Thus, staff selection provides two possible sources of poor performance. While the most obvious may be lack of capability, the second, appointing the wrong fit, may be equally problematic. In some ways this is more difficult to deal with because such poor performance is then not due to lack of individual capability but to a lack of appropriate outcomes, despite what in other circumstances might be appropriate skills. If the 'fit' isn't working, it has to be resolved by changes in the employee, the situation or both or by the employee moving on to a more suitable position (see the example of Alice in Chapter 8).

The interview should also be the occasion when the candidates assess whether they feel they have the skills for the particular post and, in the circumstances, are likely to be successful and also whether they wish to work in the school where they are being interviewed. There needs to be a match between staff selection and staff acceptance. A summary is given in Table 2.1 below.

Induction

While it is generally recognised that new employees need some sort of initiation into their new organisation, this is usually envisaged as a rather basic introduction to people and procedures. In teaching, this also tends to be associated only with those who are obtaining their first teaching post. For some reason, those beginning their second or subsequent teaching posts and teaching support staff are seen to need only the most rudimentary introduction to their new job. Both these assumptions are the source of poor functioning and represent a missed opportunity.

New staff often replace highly regarded staff who have gone on to promo-

Table 2.1 Problems arising from poor staff selection

Potential problems	Results
Key skills of job not identified	Lack of capability
Candidate's skills not matched to job	Lack of capability
Poor fit between candidate and school culture	Capable employee performs poorly

tion, and the change is hence often seen as an inconvenience rather than an asset. Commercial organisations recognise the cost of change in terms of the lost productivity and cost of induction which a change of staff represents. This should also be true of schools. New staff cannot initially be expected to be as productive as the experienced staff they are replacing, and it is important not to set expectations which then may lead to the new employee being regarded as a poor performer. Such initial attributions can be dangerous, as they may become self-fulfilling prophesies.

Induction has two aspects:

a   detailed factual introduction to the new job and the new organisation
b   induction into the culture of the new organisation and its expectations

Each organisation has its own particular way of doing things. This is referred to as its culture, 'the way we do things around here'. The reasons why things are done in a particular way in a particular organisation are gradually forgotten and become habitual; however, they are consistent with some set of organisational values. They represent behaviour which values certain activities and ways of doing things rather than others. The practices indicate what is regarded as important. While rules of behaviour may be more obviously applicable to children, there are similar but rather more implicit 'rules' for staff. These may encapsulate important values such as the way that teachers treat children   with respect, for example.

New teachers either carry on in these new circumstances in ways that have proved successful for them in the past and run the risk of making some blunders, or they try to pick up cues from existing staff about acceptable practices. If they are perceptive, they will use such cues as what is said, what is written and what practices they observe, but they will have to make inferences about why the practices are as they are.

Induction has largely been associated with the first, technical, aspect referred to above (a), with the second (b) being at best implicit. Both aspects of induction need detailed consideration for all new staff, whether or not they are in their first post. Dealing firstly with the technical aspects of operating in a new organisation, new employees need to know how things are done. They need to understand polices, operating procedures and so on. These may be collected together in a staff handbook, and are largely factual.

New staff will be different from the ones they replace. This is a great potential strength. They may provide the impetus for change and improvement. New staff also represent an opportunity to identify particular and peculiar features of the way the organisation works, i.e. its culture. They are likely to ask questions and make comments on aspects of the organisation which are different to their previous one, and can be a useful source to help highlight particular aspects of the organisation's culture and may also direct attention at inefficient practices which have gone undetected for many years, purely because they have become habitual.

So, new staff represent an opportunity to identify features of an organisation's culture. They also present an opportunity to begin to change that culture. The induction of the new member of staff offers the first opportunity to begin this process. A prime consideration will be who should mentor the new member's induction into the organisation. If no formal mentor is assigned, then how the new employee finds their way around and makes sense of the way the organisation operates becomes a matter of chance. This is likely to be as a result of asking questions of staff (and students), observing what people do, and what they talk about. They may pick up quite undesirable messages, or they may misinterpret the messages.

A planned induction tries to ensure that new staff pick up messages and seek to emulate desirable practices. Thus, the chosen mentor should be a good role model. He or she should be able to give guidance on highly valued practices and modes of operation. One aspect of culture is about giving meaning to working life and identifying that which is valued. The more this is made explicit, the less the chance of misunderstanding.

The contribution of a new employee to culture can be of two kinds. First, it may be that the culture is to be reinforced; the existing culture is to be continued and deepened. The role model presented by the mentor should be consistent with this. In this case, the role of the new employee is to fit into the existing culture. The second, and more difficult, contribution represents an attempt to influence and hence change the prevailing culture.

Such a change may be needed because currently staff are polarised into competing value systems, or the existing culture may need changing because it has become a handicap to future performance. In both these cases, the new employee needs to play their part in the change of culture. The selection process should have taken this into account in choosing the new employee, but induction is equally important in bringing about the change. The new employee represents a change and a threat. He or she represents a discontinuity, and will need support if they are not to be assimilated into the existing culture or rejected by it.

Induction needs to ensure that the new employee understands the job and its priorities. A job description coupled with regular appraisal provide the mechanisms for the discussion of changing priorities and performance. Priorities need to be set right from the start of the new job with appropriate support through mentoring. Vital aspects of performance need to be monitored so that any remedial action can be begun before any problems become high profile. This should cover both aspects of performance that need improvement and also aspects of the job which are considered important in the school but which may not be so elsewhere. In one First school, induction failed to cover the importance of classroom wall displays in that particular school. The new teacher did not notice the difference between her classroom and others, and so the problem persisted and became a noticeable feature which came to be associated with inferior performance. Consequently, this issue had to be tackled much later, when it was a much more sensitive subject than if it had been covered in the induction process. At this later stage, the teacher needed help with displays, and other aspects of performance were also causing concern. Small problems not tackled at the outset grow into larger and more serious problems. This is one aspect of the difference between good managers and poor ones. Good managers are sensitive to such small and seemingly insignificant problems and take action to prevent them becoming large problems. Failure to do so may lead to a future manager inheriting a large and intractable problem. A summary is given in Table 2.2 below.

Motivation and monitoring

Most people working in organisations like to feel that someone else cares about their work. Although there may be much intrinsic motivation to work, most people also need appropriate extrinsic motivation. They like to feel that their work is appreciated. The most difficult cases to deal with are those individuals who have been neglected and consider their work to be good and important but where such an impression may be misdirected. In fact, what they might be putting a great deal of effort into is unimportant or, even worse, actually not serving the interests of the organisation (see Example 11 in Chapter 9). Whilst there may be a few individuals who, through strong personal conviction, have particular views about what is important and are disposed to ignore the views of others, most people are willing to direct their efforts at what is regarded as the common good and any misdirection is more likely to be through lack of discussion and guidance than through deeply held philosophical conviction. Thus communication is vitally important. Primarily, this needs to be with their manager, who should be able to view their work in an overall context of the work of others in the work group rather than in isolation. Other communication will be through work groups and mentoring, if that is used in the school.

Table 2.2 Problems arising from poor staff induction

	Potential problems	*Results*
Induction	Job not made clear	Parts of job undone
	Expectations of job not clarified	Parts of job not done sufficiently well
	Culture not considered	Candidate does not fit in

This requires that each individual knows who his or her line manager is and each manager knows whom he or she is responsible for. Many problems with poorly performing staff come about because there is ambiguity about these details. A second source of problems arises because managers do not know what staff management involves. They may not realise that they have a responsibility to ensure that their staff:

- know what they should be doing
- receive feedback on their work
- are supported when they encounter difficulties
- are encouraged to undertake training and developmental activities

Heads of department and pastoral heads who have been in post a long time may have taken on their posts when expectations were very different. So, it will not be surprising if middle managers require training which includes the current expectations of their post and provides some framework for them to work out their personal approach to their managerial work.

However, hierarchies are dependent on each level in the organisation understanding and fulfilling their role. If there are problems at higher levels, it is much more difficult for those at lower levels to play their part. However, dealing with poor performance at higher levels in an organisation is very difficult without external help. Inspections of schools carried out under the framework devised by the Office for Standards in Education (OFSTED) have recently begun to offer a way of detecting and highlighting poor performance at more senior levels.

Few posts in schools have only one line manager. The work of schools is integrated and staff generally perform more than one role and so usually work in some form of matrix structure (see Figures 2.1 and 2.2). Such structures are renowned for their ambiguity. They are created in situations where single line management is not appropriate, and so some ambiguity is recognised as inevitable. It is important, therefore, that where individuals have more than one manager it is clear who is responsible for what and who is the more senior manager and hence who, in the final analysis, is more responsible for detecting and dealing with poor performance. Failure to do this produces indecision, which does not help improve poor performance.

Examples of an organisational structure for a primary school and one for a secondary school

Individuals need informed feedback on their work. This should involve discussion about its content and also their work performance. Both are important. Staff need to be working on things that are important for the organisation, and also those things that are in their remit. The organisational structure should have allocated roles such that all the work of the

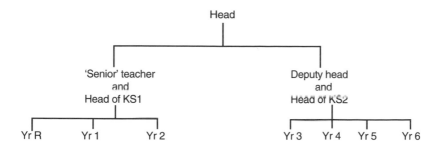

Figure 2.1 Typical organisational structure of a primary school

organisation is covered. This means that if some individuals drift into other work, a part of their essential contribution is not being made (see the example of Erica in Chapter 8).

Much poor performance is caused by complacency, which is likely to be due to lack of stimulation and challenge in the job. The prevention of this should be seen as a challenge by managers. There are a variety of ways of ensuring that staff do not fall into a rut. There are the inevitable new initiatives which schools are required to implement, but there are also periodic changes which schools themselves can initiate. For teaching staff, the timetable can be the source of stagnation or change. Clearly, changing teaching groups each year may be regarded as excessive change, but teaching the same groups for twenty years must be regarded as too static. Thus there will be some optimum period that achieves the performance improvement to be gained from repetition without the associated boredom of carrying out the same task too often. A summary is given in Table 2.3 below.

Staff satisfaction is important and managers need to know how their staff feel about their work. A checklist, based on one devised for commercial companies by the Gallup organisation to assess employees' satisfaction, asks employees to rate their organisation on the following statements:

Table 2.3 Problems arising from poor motivation and monitoring

	Potential problems	*Results*
Motivation and monitoring	Employee not motivated	Poor quality work or other interest taken up
	Work and standards not discussed	Job not done or not done sufficiently well

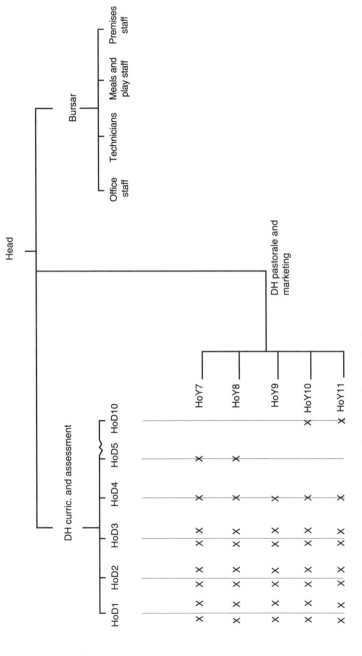

Figure 2.2 Typical organisation structure of a secondary school

Key
DH   deputy head
HoD   head of department
HoY   head of year
X   member of teaching staff

1   I know what is expected of me at school.
2   I have the materials and equipment I need to do my work properly.
3   At school, I have some opportunity to do what I do best every day.
4   In the last seven days, I have received recognition or praise for good work.
5   My manager or someone at school seems to care about me as a person.
6   There is someone at school who encourages my development.
7   In the last six months, someone at school has talked to me about my progress.
8   At school, my opinions seem to count.
9   The mission/purpose of my school makes me feel my job is important.
10   My colleagues are committed to doing quality work.
11   I have a best friend at work.
12   During the last year, I have had opportunities at school to learn and grow.

Staff appraisal

This process should be ongoing, and formal staff appraisal should be the occasion in the year when the year's work is reviewed. This should also be the formal opportunity to talk about development needs, both from the point of view of the individual and the organisation. It is also the opportunity to review the career plans of individuals. Some developments may be planned at this stage, but it is also an opportunity to log aspirations so that as opportunities come along during the year they can be fulfilled.

While formal staff appraisal for teaching staff has been introduced, and is currently being reviewed, it is also important that non-teaching staff are included in an appropriate staff appraisal process. Many non-teaching staff work alone and provide a service. Thus they are likely to need to discuss how they prioritise aspects of their job, since they probably receive more requests from staff than they can fulfil. They may also have few indicators by which they can judge whether they are doing a good job. They are also likely to work in a matrix structure, by which they are notionally accountable to someone who is the manager of all non-teaching staff but more directly relate to a member of the teaching staff with whom they work closely.

It is essential that if there is poor performance then this is included in appraisal. This should be the formal starting point for tackling poor performance. However, poor performance which is of a short-term nature should not be left until the next formal appraisal before being tackled. The other situation which is unlikely to wait until the next formal appraisal is if a new manager comes in and becomes aware of performance which is not acceptable to him or her, based on previous experience (see Example 11 in Chapter 9).

In this book, poor performance includes inadequate performance caused by lack of competence and also poor performance caused by organisational factors. Where it is a case of refusal to do an acceptable job, then this is a disciplinary matter. Dealing with poor performance is covered in detail in other chapters and will not be pursued here. A summary is given in Table 2.4 below.

Staff development

Staff development can be achieved either through staff attending training courses or through planned experience. Training courses can involve attendance at off-site courses or in-house training courses. Off-site courses which involve working alongside staff from other schools have the merit of preventing staff from becoming too insular. On the other hand, on-site corporate training, such as INSET days, can have an advantage in terms of exposing all staff to the same stimulus, and also for team building. Thus both types of training have their place.

Complementing training is the process of learning from planned experience. This involves a member of staff taking on a new task and working with the aid of a mentor on the task. The mentor's role is not to tell the member of staff how to carry out the task, but to ask questions and act as a sounding board so that ideas are systematically considered and learning takes place as a result of the experience. All of these forms of learning are valuable and each has its place, so it is a matter of choosing the appropriate training or sequencing from the above forms of development to achieve maximum learning.

Development should precede any new initiative being introduced to a school, and should also be accompanied by ongoing support as the initiative is implemented. Any new task for an individual or the school as a whole should automatically be expected to involve familiarisation and some form of preparation for the new task, rather than just assuming that professionals will cope. Using a readiness and capability chart to assess the attitude and

Table 2.4 Problems arising from poor staff appraisal

	Potential problems	Results
Staff appraisal	Work problems not discussed	Job not done or done sufficiently well
	Career plans not discussed	Employee not motivated or has to devise own career path unaided
	Needed development not discussed	Lack of motivation or lack of skill for school changes
	Employee problems not discussed	Frustration

competence of each member of staff for the change can help tailor the development necessary for each individual rather than treating everyone as the same. Development is also valuable where a new headteacher or manager wishes to raise standards or otherwise influence the culture of a school. The setting of new expectations and reinforcing these through training and development helps prevent misunderstanding and ensures that all staff are familiar with the new expectations. It is then easier to go on and deal with deviations from expectations which have been made clear. A summary is given in Table 2.5 below.

Exit interview

When a member of staff leaves, an exit interview provides an opportunity for him or her to talk about the job and its constituent elements. The particular skills which staff consider necessary for successful performance of the tasks can be discussed. This both clarifies the actual job as undertaken by the member of staff, and also begins to assemble a job description and person specification for a replacement.

Investors in People

Many schools have found Investors in People (IIP) a useful vehicle for ensuring that all the staff in a school are covered by all the elements of the management of staff. This includes all staff understanding their contribution to the aims of the organisation, having an appropriate job description and being developed to do their job well. Schools can use the IIP checklist as a means of reviewing their processes of staff management.

Table 2.5 Problems arising from inadequate staff development

	Potential problems	Results
No development	Unskilled for future changes	Shows lack of competence in school development
	Lack of professional progress	Little stimulation to improve
	In a 'rut'	Quality of work gradually falls or fails to match improvement of other staff

Chapter 3

Poor performance and its causes

Introduction

This section has been written in general terms to cover poor performance from any of the employees of a school: teachers, classroom assistants, clerical, technical or caretaking staff. Schools should have procedures for providing help to any poor performers. While these may be codified in professional support procedures for teachers, similar principles should be applied to other employees; thus, the suggestions contained in this section should be of help in dealing with any poor performer.

This section deals with:

1 What is poor performance?
2 What are the most common means by which it is discovered?
3 Is it likely to be more noticeable now?
4 Does it have to be tackled?
5 Who should notice it and take action?
6 What are the stages involved in dealing with poor performance?
7 What are its possible causes?

What is poor performance?

Any evaluation of the work performance of an individual will identify good aspects and poorer aspects. Even the best-performing employee will have aspects of his or her performance which are poorer than the others. However, what we have in mind for the 'poor performer' is someone whose overall performance is below that which is satisfactory. We believe that the most basic and implicit evaluative component in any appraisal process is an overall judgement of the work performance of an appraisee as 'competent' or 'not competent'. This is an overall judgement on competence, not one of individual aspects of performance. The basic question is, 'Is this person performing the job to a generally acceptable standard over most of the important areas within the job?' For a teacher, this would involve a consideration of their teaching with most of their groups. Inevitably there will be points of improvement, but this initial question is concerned with the standard of teaching with most of the groups taught and its general adequacy.

Thus, to make this quite clear, in the case of teachers, we do not mean the poorest teacher in the school, since there will always be one teacher who is slightly less good than the others. In our terms, it is perfectly possible that a school has no 'poor performers', in the sense that all teachers are basically competent. It is equally possible, especially in large schools, that there may be more than one teacher who is a 'poor performer'.

The term 'poor performers' is used here for any employees who are less than competent over large and important areas of their work. However, there will be many others who have individual aspects of their work performance that need improvement. Such individual aspects of poor performance are probably best tackled in a joint problem-solving mode during an appraisal process, but this section should also be a useful source of ideas for investigating the causes and ways of improving aspects, such as dealing with paperwork, time management, improving techniques with particular groups, and so on.

What are the most common means by which it is discovered?

Evidence of poor performance can arise in a variety of ways but the most frequent are:

a   OFSTED school inspections
b   parental or other formal or semi-formal complaints
c   performance gaps in exam results or other performance criteria
d   perceived problems
e   staff appraisal

While one of these may be associated with the final identification of the problem, there may have been earlier indications by other means. It appears that in a great many cases, whilst there may have been multiple signals, there is one final trigger which precipitates action. In cases of long-standing poor performance, it is often the arrival of a new head or other senior manager who makes a clear identification of an unacceptably poor performance. It seems that existing senior staff have become habituated to this level of performance as a tolerable norm.

OFSTED school inspections

Since 1993, formal school inspections carried out by contracted inspectors following a framework laid down by the Office for Standards in Education have been carried out in every state primary, secondary and special school. Such inspections involve a team of inspectors observing teaching and other aspects of a school's work over a one-week period. The inspection report covers:

- the quality of education provided by the school
- the educational standards achieved by pupils
- the efficiency with which the financial resources made available to schools are managed
- the spiritual, moral, social and cultural development of the pupils

Since 1996, all teachers have been graded on a seven-point scale, where grades 5 and below represent unsatisfactory performance. The assessment of teaching performance involves observation of teaching performance and takes account of:

- teaching quality
- response of pupils to lessons
- attainment of pupils in relation to national standards
- progress made

Each teacher is informed of his or her overall assessment and the headteacher is informed of the gradings of all teachers. Thus staff who are graded 5 or below are brought to the headteacher's attention and the proportion of unsatisfactory lessons observed during the whole inspection is stated in the written report. Such evidence needs further investigation, and it should not be taken as definitive. Research indicates that such judgements by inspectors do not always coincide with the judgement of headteachers of their staff's performance, and inspectors do not always agree with each other's gradings (Fidler *et al.* 1998).

Complaints

The final trigger for a great many cases of poor performance is a more or less formal complaint. Often this is a written complaint about a teacher from parents, but it may also be a verbal complaint. Rarely does this come as a complete surprise. Usually either there are some suspicions or, often, the problem has been accepted but there has been a lack of will to do anything decisive about it. Such a formal complaint often galvanises action.

It is our impression that complaints to schools about the progress of children and the performance of teachers have become more numerous. The reasons for this are far more complex than to suggest that this signals any deterioration of teaching performance compared to the past. As a whole, parents have become more conscious of their 'rights' and show a greater willingness to complain. The government and others have stressed the importance of education and have led parents to expect that their child should make progress while at school. There have been cases where parents have taken schools and LEAs to court for their failure to educate children appropriately or to stop bullying.

In addition to a professional duty to respond to any complaint, schools are now under pressure to attract and retain pupils if their income is not to suffer. Any complaints represent dissatisfaction which may affect not only the pupils concerned but may become more widely known and cause the reputation of the school to decline.

Performance gap

Performance information on schools has become more widespread and public. Thus the overall performance of children in a school can be compared with similar statistics from other schools. The publication of this data was intended to influence parents' choice of school. This has led to increasing analysis within a school of the results of groups of children which contribute to these overall figures.

Such internal analysis of examination results needs to take account of the initial ability of the children in a particular teaching group if it is to be used as one measure of the performance of a teacher. For GCSE results, there are ways of comparing the performance of children in a particular teaching group with the performance of the same children in all their other subjects. This gives a fairer comparison of the performance of different teachers.

Examination results are an important outcome measure of schooling, but there may also be internal process measures which also throw light on particular aspects of staff performance. These could range from pupil attendance data and the number of pupil punishments by individual teachers to the spending of delegated budgets by heads of department. Clearly all such data should be sensitively used, but they can be an objective pointer to a potential problem.

Perceived problems

Many cases begin with a general feeling that there are some signs of a problem. These may be no more than straws in the wind and often are not investigated further unless there is some additional trigger. Some illustrations are: excessive noise from the classrooms of certain teachers; certain support staff never seem to be very busy; the caretaker is often not to be found. On investigation, it may be found that there is a perfectly acceptable explanation for the symptom and that there is no problem. Often, however, these are signs of a deeper and more serious problem.

Staff appraisal

Our impression, supported by evaluations of the working of the staff appraisal process for teachers in schools, is that formal staff appraisal has not, so far, been a major source for highlighting poor performers. Partly this may have been because fewer appraisals have been carried out recently, pending a reform of the appraisal process for teachers, and partly this may have been because the purely developmental approach which was generally adopted for the first round of staff appraisals led to many such problems being ignored.

Is it likely to be more noticeable now?

There are a number of reasons why poor performers present a greater problem than in the past:

- in the context of school improvement there is now greater scrutiny than ever of the performance of a school – inspection, league tables, and improvement targets – and every member of staff contributes to the performance of a school;
- school inspection reports and high-profile statements by the Chief Inspector of Schools have contributed to a situation where there is less tolerance of poor performance in schools, and this is reflected more generally in employment practices outside school;
- parents in particular are now more critical of poor teaching and, as a school's income depends upon the number of children in a school, retaining parental confidence is very important;
- changes brought about since the Education Reform Act of 1988, and which have continued and appear to be intensifying, are likely to have exacerbated some problems of poorly performing teachers and others by increasing the demands upon them;
- delegated, tight budgets mean that a school in which there is poor performance is wasting resources which could be deployed in other ways.

In response to these concerns, the government negotiated revised capability procedures with teachers' unions in November 1997. These were intended to clarify the timescale for support activities for poor performers (expected to be no more than two terms) and also introduced a so-called 'accelerated procedure' in extreme cases for speedily removing any teachers where 'the education of pupils is jeopardised'.

Does it have to be tackled?

There is probably no ideal time to deal with poor performers, and there will be an inevitable temptation to regard the situation as less serious than it warrants, or only temporary. Unless there is a great sense of urgency dictated by the situation, there will be a tendency to postpone action until a better time. A further reason for inaction is that the consequences of action appear to be somewhat unevenly balanced. On the one hand, there is the poor performer who is likely to be very deeply affected by any action, while on the other hand, there are others in the school – children, teachers and other staff – who may be affected but to a much lesser degree (see the example of George in Chapter 9). This is the very human face of poor performance. Thus it takes a great deal of resolve to tackle poor performance.

Among the principal reasons why action is needed are the following:

- further groups of children will be denied their fair share of educational opportunities, and children have this opportunity only once;
- staff generally expect that something will be done about those who are failing to do a proper job;
- parents and the general public lose confidence in a school, and education more generally, if it does not deal with those staff who are known to be performing inadequately.

If it is accepted that something must be done, then the real issues are related to how to tackle the problems fairly and with consideration to all concerned. It is likely that those who are not doing a good job do not really enjoy their work and may only persist in schools because they feel trapped. For poorly performing teachers there is life outside teaching, and it is possible to have a very successful career outside schools and colleges.

If this sounds rather final and pessimistic, this is only because it should be faced at the outset that for a small fraction of the small number of staff who are poor performers, it may be in everyone's long-term best interest for them to leave schools. It is a sign of good management if this can be accomplished firmly but with the minimum of pain and anguish.

While this may be the ultimate destination of the very few, this should only happen after genuine and positive efforts have been made to investigate and solve the problems of poor performance. Not only is this required of ethical managers, but it is also backed up by employment legislation.

Conscientious managers will wish to ensure that they are getting a true picture of the performance of their staff, that they fully consider the reasons for any poor performance, and that they engage with the poor performer in a positive and firm but supportive way in tackling the poor performance. For these and other reasons, it is important that when poor performance comes to light it is investigated, and if substantiated, pursued. From a legal point of view:

The longer an employee remains in post, the more difficult it becomes to argue that he is incompetent. It is vital, therefore, that indicators of incapability are investigated immediately.

(Drummond 1990: 85)

Who should notice it and take action?

As we have indicated above, some cases of poor performance may be brought to a school's attention. It would then fall to the headteacher to set up processes to investigate and, if poor performance is substantiated, to take action. However, poor performance of staff being brought to a school's notice is far from an ideal situation. A school would be seen to be reactive; the timing of any action would not be of the school's choosing; and any action would be more public than might be desirable. For all these reasons, a school should have systems of management in place which are capable of detecting and acting on poor performance in a more proactive way before there are external complaints.

A comprehensive organisational structure is needed which ensures that each member of staff has a principal manager and that managers are aware that in managing staff they have some responsibility for their performance. In such a case, it is then clear who should be responsible for monitoring performance and initiating action when there is a gap between desired and actual performance. As Chapter 2 on managing staff makes clear, staff management involves more than monitoring the work of staff to detect poor performance, but it is that aspect which we highlight here.

In addition to these structures and expectations, each school needs to set up a policy for dealing with poor staff performance. By clarifying what is understood by competent performance, any departures from it should be easier to identify. The policy should also cover details of what procedures should be followed if a manager encounters poor performance.

Temporary, recently discovered and long-standing poor performance

One classification of poor performance is based upon the recency of its discovery. Poor performance may either have been discovered only recently, or it may have been known about for a long time. Recently discovered poor performance may be of two types: it may be a temporary problem with a clearly identified source which can be speedily dealt with, or it may be a serious and more difficult issue which has only just been discovered.

Temporary. We use the term 'temporary' for problems of staff performance which have recently been identified and where previous performance has been satisfactory or better and there is a clearly identifiable cause.

Recently discovered. We use the term 'recently discovered' for cases where a serious case of poor performance has just come to light. This is most frequently encountered in new staff when there is no record of previous good performance in the present job from which the current performance can be seen as a departure.

Long-standing. We use the term 'long-standing' for performance which has been poor over a long period, whether or not this has been dealt with previously. In such cases, we do not consider that poor performance has really only been 'recently discovered' when there has been a recent triggering incident that has brought the issue into prominence but where the poor performance has none the less been known about in some form for some time.

We believe that these are important distinctions because we have found that they have implications for the severity of the problem and the difficulty of dealing with it. They also have implications in terms of who is most likely to be dealing with the problem. We have found the following general associations between the discovery of the problem and the manager who is dealing with it:

- temporary and recently discovered poor performance tends to be dealt with by the person's existing manager, generally with more senior support;
- long-standing poor performance tends to be dealt with either by a new headteacher or by a new middle manager with a mandate from the existing or new headteacher.

More recently, we have observed long-standing poor performance being tackled by existing managers when under pressure from, or thought to be under pressure from, external sources such as OFSTED inspectors or parental complaints.

What are the stages involved in dealing with poor performance?

Although these stages are discussed more fully in the next chapter, it is important at this juncture to gain an overview of the whole process. The stages are:

- diagnosis
- agreement on specific improvements to be made
- provision of support and help to make these improvements
- monitoring and review of progress on improvement
- change of job, voluntary departure or dismissal if this fails

The process of diagnosis is a crucial one. Diagnosis has two functions:

1   to investigate allegations of poor performance, to substantiate them or to show them to be ill-founded;
2   to begin to formulate tentative hunches about the causes of poor performance if it is substantiated.

While the next chapter takes up the practical details of diagnosis, the remainder of this chapter provides some theoretical insights into possible pitfalls in the process of investigating poor performance and offers a classification for 'difficult' people. The process of investigation should aim to accumulate as much factual evidence as possible. This can then be separated from opinion and judgement. Where possible, evidence should be drawn from multiple sources and involve as many forms of data as possible.

It is all too easy to slip from a factual description of what happened into inferences about why the situation developed without realising it. We can observe and faithfully record:

• what people say
• what people write
• what people do

Anything beyond this is inference. Why people do things is a matter for speculation. Even what they give as their reasons may be a poor guide to their 'real' reasons. In drawing valid inferences, we look for patterns of consistency on the basis that we are less likely to be misled about true motives if there is a consistent pattern. However, it should be remembered that there is still a chance of error even in this case. The next section tries to guard against stereotyping and suggests more valid means for judging performance.

Attribution theory

There are dangers of misperception of both behaviour and its causes. An article by Mitchell and Green (1983) looks at attribution theory to gain insights into how poor performers are diagnosed, as well as the perceived causes of their poor performance. A systematic attribution process consists of:

1   observe action
2   infer intentionality
3   make attributions about internal or external causes of the action
4   respond in light of the attribution

The causes may lie within the individual (internal) or they may lie in the job or its context and surroundings (external). Any solutions proposed will differ depending upon whether an internal or external attribution is made. An internal attribution should lead to changes in the individual while an external one should lead to attempts to change the job or environment

Three kinds of information are used to assist in diagnosing whether the causes are internal or external:

- distinctiveness: differential poor performance in some aspects of the job compared to other aspects is more likely to lead to external attribution
- consistency: how has performance changed with time (more likely to be internal if it is a similar pattern)?
- consensus: is performance similar to other people doing the same job (if so, an external attribution is likely)?

In addition to the internal/external distinction, a further distinction is necessary between stable and unstable causes; that is, whether there is a clear pattern over time. For an internal attribution, if the pattern is stable then the cause is likely to be seen as lack of ability, while an unstable pattern is likely to point to lack of effort. For an external attribution, a difficult task would cause a stable pattern while bad luck might be seen as the cause of an unstable pattern.

There are two systematic biases to beware of when making attributions:

- *actor/observer bias*: this assumes that other people have internal causes of poor performance while external factors affect oneself
- *defensive attributions*: this assumes that one's successes are due to personal internal factors and failures are due to external factors, and vice versa for other people

Some social factors also appear to affect attribution.

- *leader subordinate relationship*: if the poor performer is similar to the leader or the leader is familiar with the job then the cause is more likely to be attributed externally, while if failure reflects on the leader then an internal cause is more likely to be attributed

There is some evidence that the separation of behaviour and its effects is difficult. If the same behaviour has disastrous consequences, then more extreme actions are likely to be taken than if the consequences were small; for example, carelessness with matches leading to a smouldering wastebin compared to the school burning down.

Internal causes are generally diagnosed and seen as easier to change than external ones. Mitchell and Green (1983: 513) conclude: 'Leaders are likely to attribute the cause of subordinate failure to internal motivational causes.'

They suggest that this is frequently an incorrect attribution and suggest that understanding the attribution process can lead to more correct diagnoses.

Latham *et al.* (1987) point out some other biases to beware of when observing and rating performance:

- *Contrast effect* is concerned with the tendency to rate performance in comparison with that of others rather than on absolute performance in the specifics of the elements of the job. This leads to inaccurate assessment when the others are either very good or very bad.
- *Halo effect* leads to overgeneralisation about performance based upon one aspect which is either very well or badly done. Each individual part of the job performance needs to be considered individually and independently.
- *Similar-to-me error* involves the tendency to inflate the assessment of the performance of those who are similar to oneself in outlook and attitudes and underrate those who are very dissimilar.

Diagnosis involves gathering evidence. This may be hard data but it may also be soft data – impressions, hunches and surmises. Both kinds are valuable but the softer kind should always be regarded as provisional until adequately confirmed. The evidence of behaviour should be accumulated over as long a period as possible so that present performance can be seen in context. This may show a sudden drop or a gradual fall or a more systematic pattern with some parts of the job being poorly done in comparison to others. It should also indicate some areas of good performance which may be the starting points for positive future developments.

What are possible causes?

If poor performance is substantiated, the next step is to investigate and begin to analyse its possible causes. The causes may lie with:

- the job and its context
- the way in which the employee has been managed
- the selection and appointment of the employee
- the employee

There is an initial tendency to assume that any cause of poor performance must reflect on the individual, but the insights into attribution above have opened up the possibility that the causes may be internal to the individual or external to the individual.

There is a further useful subdivision of internal causes: those that affect poor performance in a particular job and those which are related to behavioural characteristics which are likely to affect job performance in most jobs (and possibly social life generally). The latter may mean that while technical performance in a job is satisfactory, the ability to get on with other people is impaired. This latter group will be called 'difficult people' (Bramson 1981). This group will be considered last as they are only partially related to poor performance.

It is worthwhile to further divide external causes into those that are situational – the job and its context – and those that are process related – how individuals are managed. This section considers external factors first since these should be taken into account or eliminated before going on to consider the individual.

Job and its context

It should be faced as a possibility that not all jobs can be done satisfactorily. Where a job has been done by previous incumbents satisfactorily, and providing the job has not changed and the previous occupant was not especially talented, then there may be no doubts about the job. However, where the job is a new one or has substantially changed, the possibility of an 'undoable' job should be considered. The crucial question is, 'How do I know that this job can be done to the standard that I consider satisfactory?' Many teachers' jobs have changed as a result of the Education Reform Act, and thus individuals are being asked to do jobs in ways which they have never previously been done. Many middle managers' jobs have accreted additional tasks along with a growing recognition of how much more there was to the original job. Thus to be asked to do a new, enlarged job to what is increasingly recognised as an appropriate but higher standard sets new and higher levels of competence and these may be unattainable for previously competent performers without other adaptations; for example, more time in which to carry out the duties or more clerical or other assistance.

Most jobs have elements that are difficult, either by their very nature or because time pressures make them so. An organisation which is continuously striving to do better should be constantly on the look-out for such elements, which can be made less demanding by redesigning the jobs in some way. There is no merit in making life difficult on the basis that previous groups have surmounted such obstacles and that this is in some way meritorious. There are enough real problems without artificially adding to them problems that can be prevented or designed out.

Mager and Pipe (1990) suggest considering whether there are features in the context of the job which militate against good performance. They suggest considering such questions as:

* Is performance punishing?
* Is non-performance rewarding?

- Does performance really matter to them?

These really revolve around the proposition that individuals may well operate in their own best interests as they interpret them in the context of the particular job. It really is quite unreasonable to expect anyone, even teachers of great professionalism, to be able to calculate what is best for the school and to carry this out when all the effects of carrying out the particular job in its context are unpleasant or appear punishing or that not doing the job is more pleasurable. Getting some teachers to do more of a demanding job can make good performance a punishment, while letting off those who find some aspects of the job a struggle is to reward non-performance. Completing paperwork on time is a typical example. This is not to suggest that those with a natural ability for a task should not be given more of it to do, but rather to suggest that this should be seen as an explicit trade-off for being relieved of some other work.

The basic principle is that the organisational messages while carrying out the job should be clearly reinforcing successful performance rather than ambiguous. Clearly delegated jobs for which individuals are correctly prepared and equipped and for the performance of which they are accountable and rewarded provides the basis for performance mattering to individuals.

Management

The way in which individuals are managed in the job can have a profound effect on their performance. While an element of this is the elusive capacity to lead and motivate other people, there are much more mundane, but nevertheless important, processes such as induction, coaching, training, communication and praise which are vital to the successful performance of others. In cases of poor performance, the operation of these processes should be investigated to see if their lack or poor operation is a major contributory cause of poor performance. Clearly any lessons should be learned for the future. It is much more difficult to change habituated poor performance than to ensure that appropriate standards of performance are started and maintained when a new employee starts or an existing employee starts a new job. Induction, training, coaching and supervision are the essential ingredients to starting an employee in a job successfully.

Where good management practices are operating – suitable people have been selected for jobs, have been appropriately inducted and have begun to work competently – diagnosing cases of subsequent poor performance is much simpler. Any fall-off in performance can be recognised as a change from previous practice, and the range of possibilities is likely to be reduced to personal changes affecting the employee or possibly changes in the job. Any personal factors affecting the work performance of the employee should be picked up and appropriate counselling procedures used.

The individual

When other possibilities as whole or partial contributory causes of poor performance have been considered, there remains the contribution of the employee. As indicated earlier, it should not automatically be assumed that the problem only lies with the employee, but few problems do not have an employee component.

The first big distinction to be made is between those problems which represent a deviation from previously satisfactory performance and those which are associated with a long history of poor or difficult performance.

Recent effects

If the employee has been performing satisfactorily until recently, then the more profound causes of poor performance considered in the next section are unlikely to be serious contenders and the most likely cause is some personal or social effect on the employee. The cause of these effects may lie at work or, more likely, outside work.

Stress can affect performance considerably, either directly by a failure to concentrate on the job or, more indirectly, by reducing the importance of work compared to the cause of the stress. Personal causes of stress are often linked to health worries or medical conditions. Social effects are likely to involve relationships with others and issues concerning family or friends. Often such causes may have to be inferred until the individual is willing to talk about the problem.

There are two kinds of more severe psychological disorder: neurosis and psychosis (Stewart and Stewart 1982). Neurosis is when the patient knows they are ill (and is more common). Typical conditions are anxiety, depression and obsession. Psychosis is when patients do not realise they are ill but other people often do. Typical conditions are paranoia, delusions and withdrawal. The clues to psychosis are sudden changes, inactivity, capriciousness, sudden increase or decrease in speech, extreme emotionality, tremor or persistent sweating. A change in these is a better indicator than the actual level of them, since there are differences in individual's base levels of these behaviours. In such cases, and also for alcoholism and drug abuse, Stewart and Stewart recommend that all the manager should do if any of these are suspected is to create the circumstances for a talk and create an awareness of the need for professional help.

Long-standing effects

In cases where the poor performance has been the condition for some considerable time, or where the person is new to the job and has not demonstrated satisfactory performance, the considerations need to be much more penetrating. It should not be taken as self-evident that the person has the appropriate intellectual or other skills for the particular job.

It may be that the original selection process was flawed. The whole purpose of a selection process is to identify those individuals with the intellectual, behavioural and other skills appropriate to a particular job. In the main, any evidence for these skills before appointment will relate to a different job in a different context, and so it is a matter of inference that the person will be able to do the present job satisfactorily. These judgements may be just plain wrong. Any evidence for a mis-appointment should come from the induction process and follow-up. The appropriate question to ask so as to examine whether this is a possible cause is: 'Could they do it if their job depended on it?' (Mager and Pipe 1990). Where a mis-appointment was made a long time ago things are very difficult. In hindsight such problems should never have been allowed to happen, but as Honey (1980) relates:

> the substantial ones almost slip into being. They develop over a period of weeks, months or even years. Initially the problem does not seem worth bothering about and, before we know it, it has settled down into a predictable pattern that looks obstinately permanent.
>
> (*ibid.*: 6)

If the answer to the question is that the person is capable of doing the job, then the two possibilities are that they don't know how to do the job or that they don't want to do the job. The first case is a training/induction/coaching problem, while the second is a motivational problem. Stewart and Stewart (1982) point out that for new employees there may be very basic needs which require satisfying, such as feeling secure and obtaining satisfactory accommodation, before the newcomers can really wholly concentrate on the job.

Difficult people

These people are not necessarily poor performers in a cognitive sense but are poor performers behaviourally when they work together with other people. Bramson (1981) has identified seven stereotypes. Actual examples are likely to be composites of these seven:

- *Hostile-aggressives*, who bully and overwhelm by bombarding others, making cutting remarks or throwing tantrums when they do not get their own way.
- *Complainers*, who gripe incessantly but never try to do anything about it either because they feel powerless or will not accept responsibility.
- *Silent and unresponsives*, who are monosyllabic.

- *Super-agreeables*, who are often very personable, funny and out-going individuals. They are reasonable, sincere and supportive while you are there, but left to themselves they don't deliver.
- *Negativists*, who will pour cold water on any new proposal.
- *Know-it-all experts*, those people who think they have superior knowledge and wish others to recognise it. They are condescending if they have genuine expertise and pompous if they don't.
- *Indecisives*, those who stall on major decisions until they have no choice or who hang on for the perfect solution.

Bramson maintains that such people have possibly unconsciously learned these behaviours as a means of manipulating others. They all have the effect of putting others at a disadvantage.

Chapter 4

Dealing with poor performance and a range of solutions

Introduction

The stages of dealing with poor performance include the following:

- diagnosis
- agreement on specific improvements to be made
- providing support and help to make these improvements
- monitoring and review of progress on improvement
- change of job, voluntary departure or dismissal if this fails

There are further formal stages which are required for dismissal:

- governors' committee to recommend dismissal
- possible appeal to a governors' appeal panel

Throughout, the accent should be on evidence and not on opinion or, even worse, prejudice. As in appraisal and inspection, if the process of gathering evidence and agreeing the evidence can be separated from the drawing of inferences from the evidence, then this provides a sound foundation for all future efforts.

Five useful questions to ask about poor performers, based upon those suggested by Mager and Pipe (1990), are the following:

- Do they know what they should be doing?
- Can the job be done by a normally competent person?
- Do they have the skills to do it?
- Could they acquire the skills?
- Could they do it if their job depended on it?

The most likely outcome of following the framework proposed here is that the poor performer improves until his or her performance is at least satisfactory. However, improvement in an unchanged job is only one of a number of possible outcomes. Others include:

- changes in supervision
- change of job
- change of school
- job redesign
- demotion/stepping down

Determination and open-mindedness

A most important decision at the start of any management of poor performance, and a very difficult one to make, is to resolve that the symptoms of poor performance will be dealt with and a successful solution will be found which is in the interests of the children being educated in the school. This should include a determination to dismiss the poor performer if it becomes necessary. At this stage, that is the least likely outcome and some might argue that such issues should not be raised lest they prejudice the process; but we argue that, at the start, it is important to have the determination to go through with the investigation and what follows. A lack of such resolution may lead to some improvement, but the extent and nature would be left to chance. If there were any resistance to improvement, any lack of resolve would be likely to be interpreted as indecision. This could lead to inertia in the poor performer or, worse, could be exploited by an unscrupulous poor performer. The resolve must be not only that improvement will be attempted but that the performance should be brought up to a satisfactory standard, since otherwise pressure to improve might cease when the going gets tough.

Such resolve provides the driving force to pursue the problem when the issues look most intractable. While there may be no perfect solution, there are almost inevitably a range of possible solutions with costs and benefits which have to be weighed up. It is important not to become too determinist about the process, particularly at the start. In most complex problems, the solution is not immediately obvious and it is important to be on the look out for potential solutions. Quite often, something emerges around which a solution can be formulated. This is not to suggest that just waiting for something to turn up is an acceptable course of action, but rather that, once the issues are identified, there may be a larger range of possibilities than there appeared to be initially. As the dimensions of the problem become clearer, so do the parameters of possible solutions.

Thus far we have said little about types of poor performance. These can be many and varied. We have assumed that lack of skill and know-how are likely to be involved. A slightly different type of issue is that of problem behaviour or what we euphemistically describe as 'difficult people'. These are people who may be technically efficient at the skill level, but it is the way in which they interact with others which is problematic. One difficulty is in deciding whether such behaviour is just acceptable individuality, or whether it is so counter-productive within the school that it cannot be allowed to continue. An employee's behaviour at work is a legitimate source of concern, but the difficulties surround the task of defining the limits to the range of acceptable behaviour and, if it is behaviour of long standing, and characteristic, how might it be changed? For the remainder of this chapter, this will be regarded as just one example of poor performance which needs to be investigated according to the systematic framework described below.

Who is responsible?

The first question to be considered is who should be responsible for initially investigating and then dealing with poor performance? As we have suggested, if there is a clear organisational structure, the manager of the poor performer should be responsible.

In small primary schools this job will inevitably fall to the headteacher, since he or she is likely to directly manage all teaching and non-teaching staff. In larger primary schools where there are heads of section, either Key Stage or other units, then the appropriate section head should be aware of a problem and have made some preliminary enquiries before talking to the headteacher about the issue. In secondary schools, it will most likely be heads of department who manage departmental staff and therefore should be aware of any poor performers, while deputy heads should be aware of poor performance by heads of department or pastoral leaders.

Where middle managers are aware of a problem, have investigated and bring the problem to the attention of the headteacher, it will be clear that the problem initially concerns only one member of staff. However, when the middle manager does not fulfil this role the situation is more complex. There are three possibilities, as shown in Table 4.1.

For non-teaching staff, there should be other senior and middle managers performing a similar function to those who manage groups of teachers. Where there is a bursar or senior administrative officer, he or she would appear to be the most obvious person to deal with the poor performer or to ensure that the poor performer is managed.

What sources of evidence?

There are a range of sources of evidence which should be used in any initial investigation of suspicions of poor performance. There may be documentary evidence of various kinds. For teachers there may be pupils' results, samples of children's work and teachers' records which are already in existence.

Table 4.1 Implications of middle management failure

The middle manager is:	Implications
(a) unaware of a problem	Is the middle manager aware of his or her staff management function? Is the middle manager competent?
(b) aware of the problem but has taken no action	Does the middle manager set appropriate standards? Does the middle manager know what is expected of them? Is the middle manager competent?
(c) aware of the problem and is investigating	The middle manager is performing his or her job.

Direct observation of teaching may provide a vital source of additional evidence, while for teachers and for other non-teaching staff, evidence from other staff which helps to assemble a factual picture of the position will be important.

It is important that the evidence comes from a number of sources and indicates a trend over a period of time if a well-rounded picture of the performance of the individual and his or her working situation is to be formulated. There is clearly a danger of bias if evidence comes excessively from one quarter.

Such evidence needs to be carefully weighed up using professional judgement. The same findings may be viewed differently depending on the circumstances and whether the performance problem is temporary, recently discovered or long-standing. A normally competent performer who shows a sudden drop in performance could be expected to have a temporary problem triggered by factors external to the school, unless they were currently being asked to undertake new tasks. In this latter case, issues of skill and confidence could be involved. The investigation of a recently discovered case without a track record of previous satisfactory performance might begin from a consideration of how much evidence there was that the poor performer understood the nature of the job, its priorities and expected performance standards. It might develop into a consideration of the skills of the member of staff and their ability to acquire appropriate skills. For poor performance of long standing, there would be much more previous evidence to help place current evidence in context.

Such a weighing-up of the evidence and the circumstances may lead to a conclusion that there is no problem of poor performance of a member of staff, although there may be other issues. For example, if the problem originated from a parental complaint, it might be that the parental expectations were unreasonable. While the solution to the problem might involve the teacher, this would not be a case of poor performance as defined in this book.

At a stage which is not too premature, an interview will be needed with the potential poor performer to talk through any evidence or suspicions that have not been dispelled by the weighing-up of evidence as described above. This may identify further sources of evidence which may be needed.

Causes of poor performance and possible solutions

As the previous chapter has indicated, the causes of poor performance are many. They can be subdivided into combinations of:

- management
- the job
- the individual

As we have indicated, they should be considered in this order. When any other possible causes have been eliminated as possibilities or their deficiencies attended to, then, and only then, should the cause be accepted as the individual employee.

Although such a separation is possible in principle it is very difficult in practice to disaggregate the effects of multiple causes. There may be a domino effect by which one influence has precipitated the process of performing poorly and this has led to other things going wrong, with a resulting falling of confidence in the employee, which may in its turn cause other aspects of performance to suffer (see the example of Jane in Chapter 9). The purpose of analysing the separate aspects which have influenced poor performance in the past, and which may still be influencing it, is to try to assess what would be the effects of changing that aspect of the causes of poor performance. Since the influences may interact rather than be independent, it does not follow that if one aspect were reversed it would improve performance. As we have already said, the basic question to be asked is 'Could this person do the job if their job depended on it?'; in other words, have they got the basic capacity? This may be even more difficult to assess with any degree of certainty if the employee has lost confidence in his or her capacity because of previous external influences.

The essential question is, 'If this influence were reversed now, would the person have the capacity (with help) to respond and begin to improve performance?' There are also subsidiary questions about the rate of improvement and whether or not he or she would be able to achieve benchmark satisfactory performance sufficiently quickly.

Management

The way in which individuals are managed (or not) over a period of time can have a profound impact on the way that they do their work. Individuals who have been neglected and problems which have not been resolved over long periods can lead to a seemingly intractable situation. Often the problem comes to light when a new manager takes over, and, with some effort on both sides, a fresh start can be made.

Where an existing manager is under pressure to tackle such a long-standing problem, probably the manager's manager will need to take a hand to begin to resolve the situation. Where the existing manager is the head-teacher, and where it is accepted that there has been previous poor management of the person, some external help will probably be needed in order to begin to improve the situation.

Any improvement will take the co-operation of both parties and even where the employee has been blameless it still may be preferable for them to move to another job and start again rather than to persevere. The power of stereotyping should not be underestimated. All of us use caricatures of people in order to make sense of the world. Thus we pigeonhole people as being of a certain type. Once we have made an assessment and it has appeared to work, we are reluctant to change our view of someone. References to acting 'out of character' imply that we have formed a view as to how this person would act normally. While all of us use caricatures, there are differences in how reluctant individuals are to change their views once formed. Improved performance may not be noticed by those who are not open-minded or expecting a change. Any change which is noticed may be imputed to other causes. A fresh start has many advantages. This may mean working for another manager in the same institution, or it may require a change of institution.

We recognise that the pragmatic approach suggested above does not necessarily begin from a consideration of what is equitable from the point of view of the individual employee. Whilst we are mindful of the importance of equity for employees, we also recognise that this may conflict with the interests of children. There may be a tension between seeking recompense for what has happened in the past and the prospects of improvement in the future. We are generally persuaded by the claims of future improvement, but believe that this should only be at the expense of the employee when there is no alternative.

While a change of institution has many advantages, this may not be a feasible option for some staff because of their personal circumstances. They may be unable to move and there may be no other positions which are within travelling distance. However, even for individuals who find it possible to make a change, there are additional issues which should be faced. One such issue concerns the nature of any reference which is provided for the person hoping to change institutions. It will not be easy to convince a receiving institution that the person is likely to be successful in another institution when they have not been successful in their previous post. However, to mislead about performance in a previous post would be quite unethical. In a rational world a full explanation would suffice, but where decisions may involve a variety of individuals with differing degrees of sophistication, it should be accepted that this may not be enough.

If institutional problems have been the initial cause of poor performance, managers may feel a particular ethical need to try to change the present circumstances in order to allow the individual employee to improve his or her performance (see the example of Steve in Chapter 9). In most cases, this will be the appropriate course of action where the employee is now in a position and state of readiness to improve. The more difficult case arises when a poor performer has got that way largely through no fault of their own, but it now looks unlikely that they can respond to changed circumstances in order to improve. Here the ethical issues which suggest that the employee should receive privileged treatment should be balanced against the effects of this treatment on others, and particularly on children's education. It may be a case of balancing injustices and making hard decisions about not perpetuating injustice on others with little hope of success. In this case, where the person is unlikely to be able to improve, it may be wise to offer all help which would be required to fulfil legal obligations but no more, while accepting that there may have been injustice in the past and seeking to make amends for this in other ways than prolonging any opportunity to improve in the present post. A summary is given in Table 4.2 below.

Management of change

A particular aspect of management which also relates to the job that the poor performer is doing concerns the process of change. Change, poorly managed, can have the effect of creating poor performance. When staff are required to undertake new tasks, this should be recognised as a potential source of future poor performance. This needs to be recognised for each new change, since every change is different. Those who have successfully adapted to past changes should not be assumed to need little support through further change. Not only is every change different, but change may affect people differently depending upon their personal circumstances at the time.

Table 4.2 Possible solutions to a problem of management

Problem	Possible solutions
Management	• Improved management
	• Change of manager
	• Change of school

As those who have been in post for the last ten years will remember, each set of major changes which teachers have had to undertake has led some teachers to decide that they can no longer cope. Some such staff were supported through the changes and adapted successfully. Others had greater difficulty, and many decided that they would take early retirement. A similar reaction can be expected to any further large-scale changes. The prospect at the time of writing of literacy and numeracy hours in primary schools can be expected to provoke a similar outcome. Good supportive management can minimise such adverse outcomes.

Any substantial change for any staff should be planned. Training and skill development should be recognised as essential. The timing of such training and support should also be considered. Although some training requirements can be foreseen for any complex change, the full requirements can often only be fully appreciated when the change is underway and staff have a better appreciation of the difficulties of what is involved. The rational – ready, aim, fire – becomes – ready, fire, aim! In addition to any planned training, there will be a need for monitoring and support during the implementation of the change.

Finally, any sensitive management should be aware of individual differences. Not all staff react to change in the same way and not all will be able to take on particular changes in the same way. Thus the degree and kind of support required should be estimated for each member of staff, rather than just planned in the same way for all staff. Past failures in these aspects of the management of change may have contributed to current problems of present performance. As we have continually emphasised, good management at all levels is the best prevention of poor performance.

The job

The nature and extent of the current job commitments of an individual may mean that they are unable to carry out their work to a satisfactory standard. This fact may sometimes be obscured when the previous job holder was particularly competent or hard working and diligent, and appeared to be able to cope. It does not follow that the present incumbent of the post is a poor performer if they are not able to work as well as someone who was a very able performer. The issue is whether an ordinarily competent person should be able to perform the main aspects of the job to a satisfactory standard.

Where the total job is too onerous, then consideration should be given to removing some aspects of the job if they are not essential. Where it is not the extent of commitments which is the problem, but rather the requirement to perform one or two particular aspects of the job, the situation is a good deal more tricky. For many people, the requirement to do paperwork presents one such aspect. One view is that everyone should be required to do their fair share of such tasks, and each individual is required to be competent at this aspect of their work. An alternative view which can be explored is the degree to which some individuals are better at doing such tasks and may not even find them onerous. In this case, some redistribution of tasks could be considered whereby work is equalised as regards its extent but not all staff are required to perform the same tasks. Care must be taken to ensure that poor performance is not being rewarded with a lighter load, nor should this be left as a perception unless this is really the case and all staff concerned are happy with this as a solution (see the example of Wynn in Chapter 9).

A more inventive way of dealing with this situation is to see the job itself as being capable of redesign. Performance can be improved in more ways than merely by working harder at an unchanged job. Are difficult elements of the job inevitable, or could they be designed out? It is important here to avoid the 'martyr syndrome'. This is the attitude of mind which sees virtue in the overcoming of personal challenges, and believes that the challenges should remain so that individuals can demonstrate their virtue. The same outlook, but using different reasoning, resists change on the basis that as others have had to endure hardship in the past, present incumbents should also have to suffer. Both these views should be resisted as perpetuating poor performance unnecessarily and appealing to the more base of human motives.

The two distinct ways of improving the service given to children and young people by staff are:

1   improving personal performance standards
2   developing the job

Here improvements involve the raising of personal performance standards for an individual teacher for some aspect of the job while the job remains unchanged; for example, getting to classes on time or marking and returning work within a set time period. Developments, on the other hand, involve changing and improving the task to be done; for example, devising new ways of grouping children in class leading to improved learning, or devising a new teaching scheme for a particular aspect of the curriculum, as shown in Figure 4.1.

Changing the job may lead to greater outputs than merely working harder without changing the job. The most obvious example of a need to redesign a job or aspects of it is when 'new technology' is introduced. Few benefits are obtained if existing manual operations are performed using technology to replicate existing ways of working. Generally, far greater efficiencies can be obtained by approaching the task afresh. This begins from a consideration of how the tasks contribute to the overall work of the organisation. This contribution is then taken as the starting point and operations using new technology are devised to achieve these outcomes. Fresh thinking

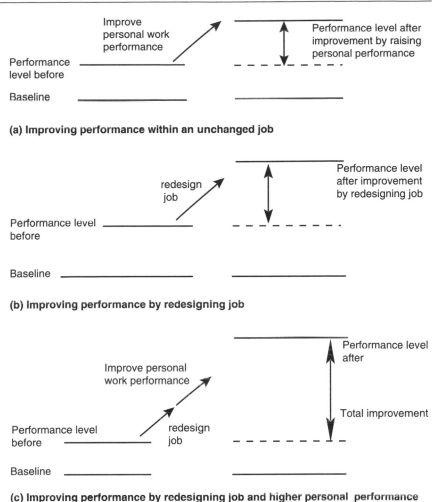

Figure 4.1 Improvement of performance and development of the job

in this way may also be able to conceive of new operations which are then made possible, and which can make a major contribution to more efficient and effective practices.

One rather small but nevertheless telling example of this is the writing of reports to parents. In some schools, this is seen as a process which must be completed by hand by teachers. However, past experience shows that if these hand-written reports are not checked then parents notice spelling and grammatical errors in the teacher's English. This leads to much senior staff time spent checking what teachers have written (if indeed senior staff can always spot such errors). Any fresh look at this process reveals it as inefficient. Some heads indeed refuse to take a fresh look at the issue and regard the process as evidence of poor staff performance.

Any consideration of the purpose of reporting to parents reveals a number of requirements, but that it should be done in the personal handwriting of teachers is not one or them. However, ensuring that the comments are personal and appropriate to their child is. Thus reporting can be computerised, but this needs to be done in a sophisticated way. It is the lack of a sophisticated approach which parents criticise when reports are computerised and many emerge with remarkable similarities. The point at issue is a more general one than computerised reporting. It is that aspects of jobs which appear problematic may not be endemic. Rather than only working with job holders to improve their performance on unchanging jobs, job redesign may well be a more successful alternative. However, for success, any job redesign may bring with it training needs so that staff can be successful in the new jobs.

A possible alternative to job redesign is job transfer. The employee is transferred to another job within the same organisation, to which they are better suited. For teachers, this could involve teaching a different age range or subject specialism, while for non-teaching staff there may be more possibilities, especially in schools where the number of non-teaching posts is expanding.

A further alternative that is not within the scope of an individual school, but which a school can facilitate, is job transfer to another school (see the example of Alice in Chapter 8). There are many examples where teachers are unsuccessful at one school but are quite competent at a different school. This may be a different type of school or a school in a different neighbourhood. Before providing suitable references, any school should be satisfied that the person is basically competent and in all probability will be able to perform satisfactorily in a new school. It is quite unethical to provide glowing references to export staff who are poor performers. In addition, if it could be shown that the reference was not written in good faith, there could be legal issues. A summary is given in Table 4.3.

Table 4.3 Possible solutions to problems with the job

Problem	Possible solution
Aspects of the job	• Training
	• Job redesign
The job	• Training
	• Job redesign
	• Change of job
	• Demotion/stepping down

The person

Most of this section is concerned with long-term problems of poor performance. However, many long-term problems begin as short-term problems which are either not recognised or not managed well. It is important, therefore, that short-term, temporary dips in performance are recognised and treated. These need to be contextualised, and so changes in management or the job which might have precipitated the problem should be considered before moving on to consider the individual. If the problem has only recently appeared, as opposed to only recently been recognised, then the cause is likely to be some recent change of circumstances. These may be connected with the individual (for example, health related) or connected with the family or home circumstances (see the examples of Roberta and Martin in Chapter 8). Other colleagues may be able to give informed guesses as to the reasons, but otherwise it is a matter of raising it with the individual in the context of effects on work. Depending on the relationship of the manager to the individual, the approach could be a personal one to raise any problems that the individual has, whereas, when such an approach is not appropriate, an approach which relates to a drop-off in work standards is legitimate in all circumstances. Often the individual is willing to talk about the issues when it is in confidence to someone they trust and who can be expected to be sympathetic and will try to help.

While tackling temporary problems can be expected to yield positive results fairly quickly the same is not generally true of recently discovered problems and particularly long-standing problems. When other possibilities have been eliminated, lack of competence in the employee should be considered, and in any case this may have been a partial cause even if there were other influences. Any solutions depend on an accurate and perceptive assessment of the nature of the problem. The earlier questions require investigation:

- Do they know what they should be doing?

While this may sound trite, it should not be taken for granted. A new manager with different expectations, gradually rising standards of expected performance over a number of years and expectations brought in from a previous job are all frequent reasons why a poor performer may not be aware initially that their performance is perceived as poor. In this case, the first step is to make clear to the person the nature of the job and expected standards of performance. Although this can be made to sound very simple and obvious, in practice it is very difficult to do successfully. The approach must be suitably pitched depending on the person and their attitudes; also, any illustration of performance standards may take a great deal of effort to clarify.

Where this exercise is required for a number of staff or where the sensitivities of the case are such that it is undesirable to single out one person, a scheme which takes the clarification of roles and expectations as a major feature can be useful. The Investors in People (IIP) scheme brings out many issues in staff management and can be used to review aspects of staff management including job descriptions and expectations for all staff. IIP may be especially useful where teaching support staff have not previously been involved in staff development activities. Although the IIP checklist can be used to review procedures, this does not necessarily have to lead on to IIP accreditation if accreditation is seen to offer few advantages.

Any consideration of how difficult it would be to instruct a novice about performing any complex task for the first time will soon reveal to those who do not think there is much of a problem about knowing what the task involves how complicated, in fact, many tasks really are.

Failure to improve, or to improve adequately after this step has been taken, leads on to the next question. Although the questions are sequential it does not follow that they have to be considered independently. They should all be considered at the beginning. However, although preliminary answers may be formulated at that time, it may be that, as further evidence becomes available, the answers need to be reconsidered.

• Do they have the skills to do the job?

This requires a clear specification of the skills needed to do a job. This involves a consideration of ability, experience and skill development. Those who have undertaken high-level qualifications can be expected to have high ability which can be used as the starting point for further skill development. This is not necessarily true of all staff. Particularly for non-teaching posts, staff with different levels of intellectual achievement may be working side by side. It is much more difficult to assess what is possible for those who have not demonstrated high ability by previous successful study. Clearly, to be effective any skills training must be appropriate for the individual and their state of readiness.

Skill development can be achieved by a number of means, and these should not be envisaged as mutually exclusive. Generally, it is not likely to be 'either or' but rather 'and'. Thus external training courses may play some part, but mentoring and coaching within the institution are also likely to be productive.

Any skill development should have targets and timescales associated with improvement. Targets should have been formulated and the skills training and development should have been planned to be appropriate to achieving those targets by some agreed timescale. The targets should contain some means of judging whether the task is being performed sufficiently well. Targets are unlikely to be helpful for the individual worker if they do not have a clear idea of how they will be judged. If they know the criteria then they can pace themselves on these criteria. There should also be periodic feedback on performance to guide the employee.

- Can they acquire the skills to do it?

While it should be assumed that most staff who do not have appropriate skills will be able to acquire them, it should not be taken for granted that this is true in all cases. While it should be open to all poor performers to try to acquire the necessary skills, it should not be assumed that all can acquire the skills, nor that all may wish to do so. Sensitive and open-minded discussion may be needed to explore other possibilities if the two assumptions above are in question.

When the level of skill is appropriate to the job, the final question is:

- Could they do it if their job depended on it?

If the answer to this question is yes, then the problem is one of motivation. This can be encouraged positively by inducements or negatively by threats of consequences if there is no improvement. Again, it is unlikely to be either one or other of these approaches but rather combinations, in practice or implied, which are likely to be successful. However, coercive approaches should only be regarded as short term, but they may be required to get an individual started on a new way of working (see the example of Wayne in Chapter 8). For cases where the consequences of poor performance are hazardous, and for other situations, formal disciplinary procedures exist. These should be used where the situation may recur and where the job holder will not exercise skills which they have in the proper performance of their job.

Use of disciplinary procedures would not normally involve training and support since it is assumed that the person has the appropriate skills but does not use them properly. However, it is conceivable that if the lack of use is involuntary, as when an individual is under stress, then it may be appropriate to provide development to control the effects of stressful situations, if this is a contributory cause of poor behaviour for which discipline is being invoked.

When, however, the answer to the question above is that they could not, or could not repeatedly and ordinarily, do the job when it mattered to them, then this is a case of incompetence. As we have indicated above, any incompetence may have come about through multiple causes but if the analysis in this section has not thrown up any realistic means of achieving improvement, then this is a case where the person must leave the job either voluntarily or be dismissed. Clearly, other things being equal, it is much better if the person leaves voluntarily and without any sense of grievance, knowing that they have received fair treatment and that they can see and measure themselves on fair criteria which they recognise they have been unable to fulfil. While this should be the aim and is the most likely scenario if the suggestions in this book have been followed, this should not prevent the use of dismissal if the more positive scenario cannot be achieved. There will always be a few people who are unable to face up to their own inadequacies, and this should not be used as the pretext to allow poor performance to continue to blight the education of children. As we have been at pains to emphasise throughout this book, it is the interests of children which should be paramount. Schools exist for the education of children, not to provide work for teachers and others.

Dismissal should be the final option when voluntary departure has been rejected. All the stages of considering the problem and trying to bring about improvement should have involved evidence and much discussion of possibilities. Thus the poor performer should have been left in little doubt about their situation. In this case, where other posts in education have been considered and dismissed, for those who wish to continue work there needs to be an examination of occupations outside education. Here there may be interests or some experience on which to draw in terms of selecting an alternative occupation. If not, then careers advice which seeks to match interests, experience and skills to potential occupations is needed. The school may be able to help by arranging an industrial placement or other trial of potential careers.

In the past, early retirement was a much used option when other possibilities had been exhausted. There were two types:

- retirement on the grounds of ill health which could be granted at any age;
- retirement on the grounds of increased efficiency of the service which could lead to a pension being payable after the age of 50, which could also be enhanced by the granting of extra years of service for pension purposes.

Both these types have become more problematic recently. Retirement on the grounds of ill health now needs to be approved by medical representatives of the Department for Education and Employment, and is reputed to be more difficult to achieve than previously. The funding of early retirement on the grounds of increased efficiency changed in September 1997. While previously the costs of early retirement had been met by the pension scheme, from that date any costs had to be met by the employer, the LEA and/or the school.

Those who would have considered early retirement in a similar position in the past now find themselves in a much more difficult situation. It is possible for the employer to finance the costs of early retirement and LEAs, in particular cases, may be willing to consider this option but it is unlikely to be as widely available as it has been in the recent past. If this is not an option in a particular LEA, then redundancy and dismissal for incompetence are the only options if a more amicable and voluntary departure cannot be agreed.

Redundancy strictly means that the post is now surplus to requirements. Redundancy may be contested in the normal course of events and there are criteria which have to be shown to exist for the departure to be as a result of redundancy. However, if the employee is willing to consider redundancy because this is the least unpalatable option, it may be possible to arrange a redundancy situation where in other circumstances it might not wholly survive the test of redundancy criteria. This option provides a little more money for the departing staff member and has its attractions if it leads to a more voluntary form of departure than dismissal.

The final option is dismissal for incompetence. This should only come about when all the necessary procedures have been followed, both in spirit and to the letter. The employee must have been given an adequate opportunity to improve. Their failure to do so needs to be adequately documented. They should be able to appeal to an independent panel of the governing body who should fairly and impartially hear and assess the claim. Due procedure becomes very important should the dismissed employee appeal to an industrial tribunal. As the example of Jim in Chapter 9 shows, the tribunal will check to ensure that due process has been followed.

An industrial tribunal is not a means of rehearing the case. All that an industrial tribunal does is to check that due process has been carried out and that the decision that was reached was not perverse in view of the evidence. It will not attempt to challenge professional judgement except in so far as such judgement appeared to have ignored the facts of the case. Thus an industrial tribunal will:

1   ensure that the appropriate steps have been followed leading up to dismissal following capability procedures or following disciplinary procedures;
2   ensure that any decisions made were not at variance with the facts of the case.

An industrial tribunal, if it finds against the employer, may make recommendations. This, in extreme cases, may include a recommendation to re-employ the person, but is more likely to include an award of compensation. Where a recommendation to re-employ is not complied with, the court will award compensation instead. The sums awarded are generally not particularly high, but there is also the adverse publicity which follows such a finding of poor process or unreasonable decision. A summary is given in Table 4.4.

Table 4.4 Possible solutions when the problem involves the person

Problem	Possible solution
Does not know what he/she should be doing	• Explain or revise job description
	• Prioritise job description
	• Set performance standards
Does not have skills	• Training
	• Development
	• Mentoring
	• Coaching
Cannot acquire skills	• Job redesign
	• Change of job
	• Voluntary departure
	• Dismissal
Lack of motivation	• Provide an incentive
	• Coerce
	• Dismissal

Taking action

When poor performance has been diagnosed it is essential to involve the poor performer. This is important at the ethical level – 'Nobody should be identified as a poor performer without his being told' (Stewart and Stewart 1982: 93) – and also for the very practical reason that 'it's difficult to improve really poor performance…by stealth' (1982: 93). Although this generally means an individual interview with the poor performer, Stewart and Stewart suggest that if more widespread poor performance is evident on taking over a managerial role from someone else, then a standard-setting exercise for everyone is a useful precursor (see the example of Graham in Chapter 9). In this way, everyone knows the new standards of performance which are required and this eliminates any possibility of ignorance of the standard of work that is required of everybody. Investors in People checklists can be used as a device for doing this.

Counselling interview

Unless the poor performance is caused by wilful disobedience of known rules then a disciplinary interview is inappropriate. The most useful meeting is one which sets out to identify the problem and examine possible solutions. The elements of a basic framework are suggested by Stewart and Stewart:

• agree standards
• agree that there is a gap

- agree size of gap
- agree responsibility for gap
- agree on actions to reduce the gap
- agree measures and time to reduce gap
- set time for follow-up

Following any drawing together of the evidence by the manager, the poor performer should be drawn into discussions. Such discussions should focus, firstly, on shared perceptions of the standard of work performance and the adequacy of this. Jointly-collected further evidence and the judgements of others may be needed to make the case of poor performance compelling. When the poor performance standard has been accepted by the employee, the causes can be identified and plans drawn up which aim to improve performance to an acceptable level.

Such plans should commit resources and management effort for coaching and support for an agreed but limited amount of time before the results are reviewed. These plans should have the whole-hearted support of both the poor performer and manager. They should have a realistic and high chance of being successful. As the plans proceed, the closeness of working between the two people should lead to early indications of whether the plans are working. If they are working, the problem should be solved; on the other hand, if there are increasing indications that they are not, then efforts should be made to discover other more radical solutions. These should include job redesign or job change where these have not already been considered and, finally, should include the poor performer leaving the school or the teaching profession. Any examination of alternative solutions should be with the full support of the manager and the school. The school should be willing to commit resources to help find a joint solution.

Stewart and Stewart offer some useful suggestions about the approach to this interview:

- *Make it easy for the person to do what you want*: do not let the interview degenerate into a contest.
- *Handle the problem not the person*: deal with behaviour and not with personality. Not only can this be done more objectively by agreeing on the evidence but it is easier to change behaviour, and it is only behaviour at work which, ethically, a manager should wish to change. This approach is more likely to succeed since then the poor performer is not under attack as a person.
- *Deal with behaviour and results*: since the 'right' behaviour may not be producing the desired results for some reason.

By adopting a problem-solving approach it is less likely that the poor performer's response will be (taken from Latham *et al.* 1987):

- *Deny it.* This is a natural first reaction and managers should be prepared to confront it and encourage a more positive approach.
- *Hide it.* Covering up is the second response when denial would be pointless.
- *Justify it.* The next stage is to seek to justify or rationalise the behaviour.
- *Allocate it.* The problem is allocated to someone else or to external causes.

Since most problems are multi-causal, the difficulty is to know where to start on formulating a solution. Stewart and Stewart suggest: 'Find the knot that is easiest to undo, and start there' (1982: 8).

While the above represents a generalised framework that would be appropriate for non-teaching staff for which there are no further formally agreed procedures, for teachers the framework above needs to fit the revised capability procedure.

For teachers

In the revised capability procedures for teachers agreed in November 1997, there are some timescales and stages that are formally required.

1   After diagnosis, there is a formal Assessment and Decision by the headteacher. It is at this point that the following options should be considered:

- The standard of performance is not that of 'poor performance' as we have defined it. The case could be dropped or aspects of performance could receive informal counselling.
- The conduct giving rise to the poor performance is such that it should be dealt with under disciplinary procedures.
- The conduct is poor performance; further steps required.

2   The headteacher gives five school days' notice of a formal recorded interview and invites the poor performer to attend with 'a friend'. The headteacher also invites a witness to the meeting. This represents the date of entry into the formal procedure.

3   At this meeting the nature of poor performance is agreed, targets are set, a timescale normally not exceeding two terms is set and appropriate training and support procedures are agreed.

4   In the intervening period, the poor performer is given feedback on how his or her performance is progressing as the support procedures operate.

5   After the agreed period the headteacher holds a hearing to assess the results of support. At this stage formal consideration should be given if necessary to a different balance of duties or an alternative teaching post.

Dismissal

Where attempts to improve the performance of the poor performer have failed, departure either voluntarily or by dismissal should follow. For teachers this requires that the headteacher suspend the teacher and convene a Governors' Staffing First Committee to confirm the suspension and to determine that the teacher should cease to be employed by the school.

This hearing should receive evidence and make an independent decision. This either confirms the suspension and dismissal, or offers some alternative course of action. It is difficult to see how the governing committee could offer an alternative course of action without undermining the actions of the headteacher. However, the committee might take such action if it was not convinced that the poor performer had been given adequate opportunity to improve, or if the required steps in the procedure, including the appropriate documentation, was not sufficiently robust to survive scrutiny by an industrial tribunal.

Any dismissed poor performer would have the right of appeal to another independent committee of the governing body, a Governors' Appeal Hearing. It would be important that both committees of the governors acted impartially and independently of both the headteacher and each other.

Dealing with difficult people

The aim of the techniques summarised below is very modestly set at 'coping' so that the business in hand can be accomplished rather than hoping to bring about a transformation of the problem. Briefly, the analysis and suggested coping strategies for each are as follows (Bramson 1981).

Hostiles can either be very obvious in their intimidation of others or can use criticism like a rapier to achieve the same effect much more subtly. They are driven by the need to demonstrate that they are right. The effect on others is confusion or flight.

The essence of the coping strategy is to stand up for yourself and be assertive but not return the hostility. Do not show intimidation and deflect any aggression. Insist on stating your personal point of view. Be ready to be friendly at the first opportunity.

Complainers can pick on real problems but do so in ways which are unlikely to lead to solutions. They have a strong sense of how others should behave and complain when they do not do so. Generally they are powerless to do anything about it, and so the exercise is futile and demoralising for others listening to the depressing catalogue of complaints.

The key to successful coping is to break this self-confirming cycle of passivity, blaming others and powerlessness by adopting a problem-solving approach. The first step is to listen attentively; this allows the complainer to let off steam and to feel that they are being taken seriously, but it also allows the listener to await the cue to move on to the next step. Acknowledge what has been said without necessarily agreeing with it and try to make the point more accurate, since in its original form it may be rather hyperbolic. Then move on to trying to formulate the nature of a solvable problem related to the original complaint. If all else fails, ask the complainer how they would like the conversation to end.

Silent and unresponsives. Won't or can't talk when you need to converse with them. It is often difficult to understand what this means, as it is likely to be different on different occasions and certainly with different people.

Ask open-ended questions with a friendly, silent stare – a quizzical, expectant expression. Don't break the silence except to comment on what has happened and the non-response. Try to help the 'clam' out by asking helpful questions about the (silence) problem. Listen attentively.

Super-agreeables. Always tell you things you want to hear but often let you down. Promises are made in good faith but not kept. Avoidance of conflict is the highest priority, but can only be done in the short term. Eventually, when choices have to be made, someone will have to be disappointed.

Make honesty non-threatening. Try to get them to be honest. Don't allow them to make unrealistic commitments. Reassure them about their value as people. Be prepared to compromise providing it gets the job done. Listen to the humour: are there hidden messages?

Negativists. This is not the considered verdict which is a useful warning of an unsound idea but a blanket reaction to any suggested change: 'it won't work', or 'we tried it once and it didn't work'. The acid test is to ask if there are any solutions to the identified problem: to the negativist, there never are any. They truly feel dispirited and defeated. 'Negativists, with their steadfast, rational communication of helpless resentment, can touch that potential for depression in each of us and induce in us that same sense of being blunted' (Bramson 1981: 105).

Try not to get sucked in. Try a positive breakout. Try problem-solving. Try to find courses of action worth trying. Spend time analysing the dimensions of the problem and asking questions. Present a moving target. At forebodings examine the worst consequences of the course of action to show that it is less dire than imagined. Use negativists constructively and use their warnings for contingency planning. They can also prevent over optimism. Be prepared to act alone if that is the alternative to increasing depression. Some highly analytical people may act negatively until they have fully understood a situation, so don't rush them.

Examples of all of these types of people can be found among the case studies in Chapters 8 and 9.

Summary and conclusions

Poor, marginal and unsatisfactory performance may come to light at any time. Before any attempt is made to justify or rationalise not doing anything about this situation, there should be a consideration of the effects on the 'victims' of the poor performance: children being disadvantaged and other staff being demoralised.

Having decided that the problems need tackling, the emphasis should be on gathering evidence in an open-minded way in order to form a clear picture of the situation. The job that the poor performer is carrying out and its context should be studied to see if there are features which make it especially difficult. The way in which the person is, and has been, managed should also be considered to discover how far he or she will have been made aware of any poor performance and has received help to improve. Finally, the individual and their abilities and skills should be carefully considered in the light of the previous evidence. A summary is given in Table 4.5 below.

It takes a great deal of courage to tackle poor performers of long standing, but it is possible to do this positively and fairly by following the spirit of the suggestions made in this chapter.

Table 4.5 Summary of implications of different causes of poor performance

Question	Implications
Do they know what they should be doing?	Job description and supervision
Can the job be done by a normally competent person?	Job redesign if necessary
Do they have the skills to do it?	Training
What if they can't acquire the skills to do it?	Change of job or aspects of it or voluntary departure
Could they do it if their job depended on it?	Motivation or dismissal

Chapter 5

Legal and moral issues

Graham Clayton

Rights and powers

'Discipline' and employment

Though much has been done by parliament in the recent past to develop the concept of a free-standing employment right, the employment relationship remains founded in contract. A contract is, at its roots, a legally binding relationship between or among two or more contracting parties. It is terminable either by completion of the obligations agreed to be performed or in accordance with the terms, expressly stated or implied by necessity, which the contract itself contains.

Warnings by the employer that the contract may be terminated and termination itself are what we describe as employment discipline, but in reality the termination of the contract of employment is not a matter of discipline. Employers do not have the right to punish or condemn. Rather, they have that right which any party to any contract properly retains to end the contract of employment when the contract cannot be maintained for economic reasons, or when the contract can be seen to have ceased to serve the purpose for which it was created.

That 'discipline' should have survived in the language of the employment relationship against this background of law developed on the basis of respect for employee rights is startling. Certainly the law of employment will not be understood in everyday language until we abandon this notion.

Incompetence as a reason for termination

If the continued maintenance of any contract of employment ceases or fails to achieve its purpose the employer has reason to terminate the contract. If the employee's performance of the obligations of the contract is not up to a standard considered satisfactory, the overall value of the contract may be seen to be below the level required to fulfil its purpose. It is then justifiable to terminate the contract. In legal terms, we call this dismissal for a substantial reason relating to capability.

What matters most at this point is that the employee so dismissed has not been disciplined or condemned. It is the contract of employment which has been terminated because it has been found to be no longer tenable. The employee has been identified as having failed to perform adequately his or her obligations under the contract.

Once no good, always no good?

There may be many reasons for inadequacy in performance. Relatively unusual are the cases in which a teacher is found never to have been any good. Most dismissals for lack of capability follow a decline into poor performance. Anecdotal records suggest that relatively few teachers fall below the required levels of adequacy in their early career years.

Nor is every failure a failure as a teacher. It may only be a failure in a particular job, a failure to respond to a particular environment or style of leadership. It may have to do with a range of personal stresses from which the teacher can recover. It may be the consequence of failure to stay in touch with changing demands within the education service. There may be a whole host of contributing factors, and few are irretrievable.

All of these lead again to the conclusion that condemnation is not the objective of dismissal. Dismissal is the termination of particular employment which cannot be sustained. It is, in a sense, the ultimate warning. After warnings to the effect that unless there is improvement, a current employment will be lost, dismissal is a warning that without better performance in another job, the teacher will face the same consequences.

Theory, reality and mythology

This, of course, is theory. While theorising may aid understanding, there are other realities.

First, the time taken to give a teacher the chance to improve is time lost to a class or group of pupils or students. In the career of a teacher whose performance has declined, a bad year is a time from which to recover. In the education of a child or young person, it is a lost year, with potentially very serious consequences.

The opposing reality is that, though the motive in sacking a teacher should not be to condemn, that is very commonly the effect. A teacher defined as having failed is unlikely to be able to find a new teaching post without presenting himself or herself as a person reformed by bitter experience. The reality of sacking a teacher is often to force the teacher into a period of unemployment with limited prospects of reviving a professional career. It is a harsh judgement.

It is the balance of these realities which lies at the debate over poor teaching and what is to be done about it. It is the same balance which dictates the operation of the law.

The debate is one into which a great deal of false mythology has entered. It begins with commitment to the life chances of the child, a commitment naturally felt most strongly by parents. Every parent is angry and frustrated to see his or her child denied good education. So strong is that sentiment that general elections can be won and governments formed on education policies.

But for all the values of democracy, the hustings are no place for sound and considered analysis. A determination to be rid of poor teachers has instant popular appeal to those who attribute the failings of youth to a malaise in the education service. They see something of a crisis in the system and cry out for something to be done. A politician talking tough is onto a sure winner.

It is against this background that existing mythology is reinforced and new mythology created. A teacher having a bad day becomes, in the public mind, a poor teacher if that day happens to be one observed by an OFSTED inspector. Soundbite talk of fast-track dismissal heralds welcome change to the listener convinced by the frequently repeated excuse that it has been very difficult to sack teachers.

It is, in fact, no more difficult to sack teachers than it is to dismiss anyone else from employment. It is true that teachers are entitled to relatively long notice, but this is a rule established to cope with the difficulties of finding a mid-term replacement. It does not make the process of dismissal more diffi-cult and in the timescale of dealing with a case of incompetence, it makes no significant difference.

Teachers have the employment protection rights of employees, no more and no less. Dismissal must be for a substantial reason and it must be fair. The basic principles of fairness are now firmly established in the law as it relates to all employees with employment protection rights.

Much abbreviated, the principles are that an employee whose competence is in question must be clearly told of the problem as it is perceived by his or her managers, given the chance to improve, and have the benefit of reason-able measures to assist the improvement. The procedures used to deal with the problem must be fair. They must provide an opportunity for the employee to respond to complaints and be represented if he or she wishes. There are no special privileges for teachers. The law will recognise that the protection of the interests of pupils and students is a legitimate concern of the employers of teachers as it would recognise special factors relating to any particular employment.

Nor does the law provide to dismissed employees a right of appeal against the employer's decision. Industrial tribunals which consider unfair dismissal claims do not presume an employer's function. The tribunal members do not ask themselves whether they would have made the same decision in the same circumstances. They are allowed only to ask whether the employer has considered the relevant factors, whether the employer has acted fairly using a set of fair procedures, and, finally, whether the final dismissal decision is rational in response to the known facts.

The teacher organisations have no interest in protecting and defending teachers who fail in their employments. Quite apart from the principled views of members of a caring profession, the credibility of the teacher organisations and their case for improved pay and working conditions are enhanced when teaching is of high quality. They have nothing to gain from poor teaching standards.

They will, however, vigorously represent their members against unfairness and they will insist on the operation of the procedures which, in most cases, they have been party to settling. They expect their members to be given a fair chance to overcome problems, and if it is apparent that the teacher must go, their aim will be to preserve dignity and the chance, at least, of a continuing livelihood, perhaps in the form of an early pension.

Such deals are not a reward for poor performance. They are not in any event available to teachers who fail through careless disregard for their responsibilities, but such cases are rare. Reasonable settlements provide an opportunity to terminate employment with some measure of dignity for teachers who, despite their best efforts in the circumstances in which they find themselves, have ceased to be able to cope. Once the element of condemnation is removed from what we call employment discipline, settled severance is much more clearly seen as a fair option.

Management power and legal balance

Though we may be on the brink of an age of decision making by machines, for the vast majority of us, the decisions which affect us are still made by people. A decision to categorise an employee as performing poorly must be taken by a person. So must the decisions about what is to be done to address the problem.

These are management decisions taken by people whose personal qualities are such that they have succeeded in gaining status above others in the hierarchy. With this status goes the power to make demands on other people and the power to enforce those demands by threatening to deprive those people of their jobs and livelihoods.

Even those who can truly say that they actually enjoy their work rarely relish every moment of every day. Many of the demands of employment are undertaken with some reluctance. People who are not coping well in their employment are not often enjoying their work. The material benefit which employment brings to the individual is the incentive. It is that material resource which can then be spent to purchase other enjoyment.

Employees surrender a great deal of personal freedom in the bargain for material resources. They subject themselves to a high level of control and direction. They must be at stated places at stated times and they must produce results satisfactory to their employers. Most people in work place themselves under the demands of employers for around one-third of their working hours in a working lifetime.

For a very large number of people, employment involves alteration of a natural state of being. They must wake when they may prefer to sleep. They must work when they may prefer to rest. And they must accept control when they may prefer freedom of choice. We know the extent to which, in a modern society, this causes unnatural stresses.

The power to make demands on this activity is one to be exercised with responsibility, maturity and wisdom. Wages and salaries do not purchase the right to exercise power with dictatorial cruelty. We have passed through the Victorian age of labour viewed as the purchased possession of the callous entrepreneur. Employment law has matured to balance the needs of the undertaking in which people are employed with respect for the rights of the individual employee.

There remains a very strong body of opinion that the balance is still weighted heavily in favour of employers and their managers. This opinion is countered by the belief that everyone benefits from the productivity of a well-disciplined workforce, but the debate is now on the adjustment of that balance. It has long since ceased to be about whether there should be employment protection law at all. The insistence of the law is that decisions made in the exercise of personnel management powers must be the product of considered rational judgement, and not the result of prejudice or caprice.

Judgement of teachers

Criticism of teachers seems at times in the recent past to have become almost a British sport. OFSTED inspectors are charged with the responsibility of reporting on unsatisfactory lessons. In the public mind, one lesson labelled as unsatisfactory then characterises the teacher who gave the lesson, quite unfairly, as a poor teacher. Even the inspectors themselves have sometimes to be reminded that they are reporting on poor teaching which they may have observed only for an hour or so, and are not identifying poor teachers. Politicians, unwilling to acknowledge the failings of their own policies, are sometimes quite content to let teachers take the blame. Parents, exasperated by their rebellious offspring, eagerly transfer blame to teachers. For some sections of the press, teachers are favourite Aunt Sallies, whingeing lefties responsible for all the ills of disaffected youth.

In fact, of course, teaching is not a job in which one should expect to find failure. It is, for most entrants to the profession, a chosen commitment. The very large majority of teachers maintain their purpose and aim to fulfil it.

Failure to achieve that aim is only rarely the result of dismissive indolence. Many teachers who are categorised as failing obviously experience great distress not only because they see their livelihoods threatened, but also because the criticism attacks their belief in themselves. This may be a belief unsupported by actual performance. It may, on occasions, be an obstacle to a solution to a problem objectively assessed. However, a manager who fails to recognise that in commitment there may be a capacity for renewing performance, runs risks before the law. The law would certainly not accept, for example, the mass targeting of 15,000 teachers on a hit list. Nor can there be dismissals on a fast track which offends the principles of employment protection law. While politicians may sloganise and leader-writers rant, the law demands fair judgement, and it is the law which prevails.

Employment protection law is, as the phrase itself clearly indicates, about protecting employment. Though the employment relationship remains founded on the bargained exchange of payment for work, the law does now have some features more suggestive of ownership of a job, the property of the employee which cannot be taken away other than for a good reason and fairly. Unsatisfactory performance may provide a good reason for removing the employee's property in the job, but only after it has been fairly decided that the employee has forfeited the right of ownership. Employment protection is, in this sense, about the protection of property.

Competence procedures and sickness absence

It occurs occasionally that, when procedures to address performance have started or are operating, the teacher concerned goes sick. In such circumstances, it is very important to separate out the issues and to deal with them in the right context. There are three possible types of case.

Deliberate malingering

There is often a temptation to be dismissive about illness occurring while a competence procedure is ongoing and to think of it as a device to avoid the procedure. That temptation should be avoided. Deliberate malingering is a serious business. It is a form of fraud and very uncommon. It involves lying to both the school authorities and probably also to a doctor. Discovery could result in summary dismissal for misconduct, quite distinct from any ongoing competence procedure.

Obviously, deliberate malingering is not easy to tackle. Lies can only be challenged by contradictory evidence, and evidence may be difficult to come by without the kind of detective work that would not be at all appropriate in context. Unless there are very clear grounds for suspecting deliberate malingering (in which case specific advice should be sought) a doctor's statement, once received, should be believed.

Genuine illness unrelated to the competence procedure

At the other end of the spectrum of possibilities is the clearly genuine, but unfortunately timed, sickness absence, the result for example of an accident or a clearly diagnosed illness that would prevent anyone attending work in normal circumstances.

Illness related to the competence procedure

Between the two extremes is the illness which, though genuine in some cases, is linked to the operation of the procedure. The illness itself may have the same root cause as the decline in performance, or, conversely, the threat of being labelled incompetent or even deprived of livelihood may be the cause of stress which makes the person concerned ill.

Dealing with the situation

Management reaction to credible sickness absence in these cases depends, in general terms, on the stage the competence procedure has reached. While the procedure is still at the stage of assisting and encouraging improved performance, the employee's opportunity to benefit from that process should not be diminished by genuine illness. Prolonged illness may need to be addressed but through a wholly separate approach. If the illness is expected to be prolonged, the competence procedure should simply be put on hold.

On the other hand, if the potentially more punitive phase of dealing with low performance has already been entered before sickness absence begins, the employer is not forced to defer further consideration of the case by the fact that the teacher is off work. The employer should not, however, take harsher action than would otherwise be taken because the teacher is sick.

What is important at this stage is that the teacher whose continued employment has come into question should, at least, have the opportunity to put his or her point of view at any formal hearing, and there must be reasonable accommodation made for someone who is ill to do this. There is no requirement that formal hearings must be postponed indefinitely, but equally there should not be insistence that a hearing must take place on the first appropriate date even though it is plain that the teacher will be too ill to attend. It is a question of being fair to all interests in the circumstances of the case. Where the teacher is represented, it should be possible to agree fair arrangements with the representative.

Prolonged or repeated absences

Prolonged or repeated absence, though genuine, may give cause for considering whether the teacher is fit to continue in employment in any event.

There are procedures for dealing with these situations, and they should be kept separate from any competence procedure. In the same way that illness does not of itself justify a harsher penalty for poor performance than would otherwise be imposed, so should sickness not provide an excuse for terminating the employment of a teacher who is the subject of ongoing competence procedures.

In cases in which there is a link between illness and poor performance or between illness and the use of the competence procedure, it is not easy to separate the issues. The emphasis should be on trying to identify the true cause of the problem so as to overcome it if possible.

Most difficult of all are the cases where the teacher is reluctant to acknowledge illness as a cause. In the end it will be for managers in these cases to make a fair judgement between the demands of work on the one hand and compassion for the individual on the other. Advice from those who have experience in dealing with these situations will be important, and frank discussions with any union representative of the staff member concerned is likely to be valuable. Generally, they will also be experienced in achieving fair solutions to this type of case.

Problems of local management

Origins and theories of LMS

Any discussion of the personnel management of under performance in teaching has to involve a look at the oddities of relationships within the structure of local management. Governing bodies of foundation schools and their predecessors, the grant-maintained schools, though they have other problems, have been happily free of these complications.

Local Management of Schools (LMS), introduced by the Education Reform Act 1988, is an odd creation. Its great attraction was in the feeling it gave, particularly to headteachers, that they could target resources and policies according to their own school-based objectives. Though it brings with it a burden of administration to be dealt with at school level, at least it was seen as providing some greater freedom from unwanted interference from LEA politicians.

A more cynical view has been present from the outset. The cynics could not help but notice that LMS was introduced in an era of cutting public sector expenditure, and it was of course a great deal cheaper to place the government of schools in the hands of enthusiastic volunteers rather than leave it with the army of salaried local government officers. The risks of amateurism in education management were discarded while the advantages of lay consumer control were emphasised. Competitiveness as the parent of excellence was encouraged.

The voices of the cynics became louder throughout the 1990s. More and more governing bodies found themselves managing cuts, not budgets. The idea that quality would improve through competition amongst governing bodies plainly did not work, forcing the government to introduce a hugely overbearing and expensive quality control inspection system. OFSTED has now turned the theory around full circle, as inspectors are required to inspect and report on the effectiveness of governing bodies. The system is becoming gridlocked by people inspecting each other.

Conceived originally as a financial distribution and management system, Local Financial Management (LFM) very quickly became Local Management of Schools (LMS) and lost the coherence of the original concept. Statutes, regulations and orders have piled responsibility upon duty and duty upon responsibility for governing bodies.

What appears to have happened is that when ministers have felt the need to create a new duty, there is nowhere to place it except on the governing bodies. There are no other public bodies capable of accepting these statutory duties, and none at all with effective access to a workforce which can administer them.

This is the context in which governing bodies exercise employment powers. The employment status of teachers within the LMS system is, perhaps, one of the oddest, most confusing and certainly most misunderstood structures which could have been devised. It is perhaps too flattering to suggest that it was ever really devised at all, since this suggests it was actually thought through from a coherent beginning to a logical end. There are many indications that it was not. Essential features of the structure appeared before Parliament for the first time only at the tail-end of debate on the Education Reform Bill in 1988, and then only in brief explanation of a short clause enabling the Secretary of State for Education to sort the problems out later with regulations. He did so in 1989 with the first, grandly titled Education (Modification of Enactments Relating to Employment) Order, a piece of secondary legislation which has since had senior judges in the Employment Appeal Tribunal raising eyebrows in dismay and disbelief.

At industrial tribunal level, this curious Order has been the genesis of a chapter of inherently contradictory decisions. At the level of day-to-day administration, the Order gives rise to a grand mythology about who does actually bear responsibility. Given that this is the structure which must be applied in all the highly formal stages of tackling underperformance, it is hardly surprising that there is deep unease and uncertainty. All too frequently, this has one or both of two consequences. There is a huge temptation to contrive to achieve a predetermined outcome and a bullish, aggressive, determination to rush things through with fingers crossed that management will emerge from the other side of the problem unchallenged. Alternatively, the problem is not tackled at all in the hope that it will go away. When it does not, it becomes a problem for crisis management. These are the shortest routes to trouble with the law.

Evolution of employment powers

Governing bodies were placed in charge of budget. By far the greater part of the school's budget is staffing costs. Clearly, there is no point in giving governing bodies control of such a budget if they cannot decide how many staff there are to be at the school. They had, therefore, to have control of staffing numbers.

To have effective control of staffing numbers, the governors had to have the power to change the numbers even if members of staff did not wish to leave. That meant that governing bodies have to be in a position at least to decide whether a member of staff must cease to work at their school.

That is, arguably, the end of the consequences of school budget management. However, governor involvement in so-called discipline of staff was already a long-established feature of the system. The standard procedures agreed between LEA employers of teachers and the teacher unions provided for governors of county schools to hear serious disciplinary cases, with appeals then going to an LEA committee. The underlying reason for this was the belief that it was better that the first disciplinary body and the appeal body should not be from the same grouping, perhaps sharing the same loyalty. Governing bodies and LEA education committees could be seen, at least notionally, to be independent of each other.

The underlying theory of LMS was to confirm the separation of governing bodies from LEAs. The first committee/appeal committee relationship preserved a conceptual hierarchy which was inconsistent with that theory. Disciplinary powers had to be given to one or the other. They could no longer be shared. Given that governing bodies had to have control over staff numbers, with the right to cut staff from their own school budgets, it was natural that they should gain full control of wider disciplinary powers covering misconduct and lack of capability. Governing bodies of voluntary aided schools, with the full status of employers, have had this power since 1944, subject only to LEA veto.

It was not, however, necessary that the governors of locally managed schools should have these powers to complement their budgetary control. Judgement on a teacher's misconduct or professional competence is not a direct corollary of financial management, nor can this be considered a function within the expertise of governing bodies save by the chance that some of them may have relevant experience. It is difficult to find any other employment sector in which the professional competence of employees is to be judged by people who are themselves without relevant experience, nor is it right to suppose that governors were intended to do so.

The employment powers of governors of community schools

The change made in 1988/89 identified in terms of procedural steps was actually very small. In county schools (now community schools), governing body committees replaced LEA committees as the final appeal bodies in disciplinary matters. In voluntary aided schools there was no real change at all, save to remove the LEA's residual power of intervention. The newly created grant-maintained school governing bodies, inevitably in view of their separation from local education authorities, took on powers similar to those of aided-school governors.

It is the mythology created by these changes in procedure, relatively minor in form in most cases, which has given rise to so much uncertainty in the system. Like all mythologies, this one was created in stages. The simple explanation of what had happened was that all governing bodies had effectively acquired the power to hire and fire teachers. Given that these are commonly understood to be the essential features of employer status, the idea that governing bodies had become, at least, the quasi-employers of teachers rapidly became part of common understanding. Quite quickly the 'quasi' nature of governing body status, never really understood without detailed explanation, dropped out of ordinary conversation. Before long, teachers generally saw their governing bodies as their employers.

These days few teachers accurately answer the question 'Who is your employer?' Often, hidden within DfEE letters and circulars, an accurate presentation of the position may be found, but the DfEE material is not generally of great assistance on these points. DfEE circular-writers too often hide behind the term 'schools' as if impersonal structures of bricks, mortar and other building materials were magically vested with human powers of decision making and judgement.

Governing bodies of voluntary aided and foundation schools are employers of teachers. Governing bodies of community and voluntary controlled schools are not so. They cannot be. They are specifically denied the power to enter into contracts of employment. Nor are they quasi-employers. They are simply not employers of teachers at all. The features of employment which affect teachers in work far more commonly than discipline and dismissal are lacking from the relationship between teachers and these governing bodies. Sick leave and pay, maternity leave and pay entitlements, insurance, liability protection, time-off rights: all of these are the business of the LEA. Even when the governors do exercise the powers they have and bring about the dismissal of a teacher, they cannot decide how much notice must be given. This too is part of the contract of employment between teacher and LEA, and the governors cannot change it.

In fact, governing bodies of community schools have no employment powers at all save those which Parliament has conferred on them by statute.

Unlike true employers, since they cannot enter into contracts of employment, they cannot gain their authority from such contracts. Also, they cannot even direct the day-to-day work of teachers. Teachers are required to conform to the policies of the school governing body in matters in which the governing body has the authority of Parliament to make policies, but the agent for securing implementation of governing body policy is the headteacher, under whose reasonable direction teachers work. The headteacher is also an employee of the local education authority.

In strict statutory terms, there is a clear separation of powers and a clear division of roles. These distinctions have been blurred by practice, but are none the less revealed, sometimes startlingly, in the courts and tribunals. Technically, governing bodies of community schools do not even have the power of dismissal. All they can do is require the removal of a teacher from the school. That too warrants careful scrutiny. The consequence of a governing body decision that a teacher must be removed from a school is generally assumed to be automatic dismissal, but, in the words of the song, it ain't necessarily so. The consequences are actually dependent on whether the teacher is employed to work solely in one school or not. This, in turn, depends on what the teacher's contract says, and this, of course, the governors do not control.

If the contract in question is school-specific, i.e. to work in one school and one school only, it follows that when the governors make their decision that a teacher must go from the school, the contract is wrecked and it must be terminated. The governing body does not do that. The LEA does, but once the contract is wrecked by a governor's decision, the LEA plainly has no choice. It must give notice.

However, probably unknown to the draftsman of the Education Reform Act, the large majority of teachers in employment in 1988 had contracts which began:

> You are employed to work generally in the service of the LEA. Your initial place of employment will be...

When teachers holding these contracts are removed from one community school by the governing body, their contracts clearly remain viable. There is no automatic dismissal. The LEA simply removes the teacher from the school. But to where? No one knows. It is a strange limbo land. The teacher is still on the books, but with nowhere to go. What other governing body will accommodate a teacher recently displaced for lack of capability? Certainly no governing body can be forced to do so because another of their powers is to decide who is to be appointed to any vacancy in their school.

The problem has been recognised but not yet fully resolved in any precedent case. In practice, any decision by a governing body to have a teacher removed for inadequate performance is almost certain to result in dismissal simply because the finding of incompetence justifies it, but the unresolved legal conundrum none the less adds further uncertainties to the process. Foundation and voluntary aided school governors do not have these problems; they are employers in every sense.

LMS and employment protection law

Dismissal decisions by employers are regulated by unfair dismissal law. This requires that, in relation to employees who have acquired unfair dismissal protection, the dismissal must be for a substantial reason (of which lack of capability is a statutorily defined reason), and the dismissal must be generally fair. Since governing bodies of community and voluntary controlled schools are not employers, their decisions would not be subject to unfair dismissal law, were it not for a set of specific statutory provisions making them so.

The Education (Modification of Enactments Relating to Employment) Order, originally made in 1989 and now updated in 1998, is a curiosity, a sure candidate for the booby prize in the Plain English awards. Superficially, it makes governing bodies accountable to industrial tribunals for decisions they make as if they were employers.

The point of this is simply put. In reaching their decision that a teacher should be removed from their school by reason of lack of capability, governors must act without unlawful discrimination on grounds of race, sex, disability or trade union membership or activity. If their decision is one which results in dismissal, they must have acted fairly. They are directly accountable to industrial tribunals.

Not far below the surface, there are multiple problems:

1   It remains unclear whether governors of community and voluntary controlled schools are fully accountable as substitutes for LEAs as actual employers in addition to the LEAs. The 1989 Order adopted an apparently simple mechanism to achieve the desired objective. We must read the relevant employment statutes as if all references to 'an employer' included the governing body. However, the language used in the Order is the language of addition not substitution, suggesting that an aggrieved complainant can proceed in the industrial tribunal either against the governors or against the LEA, or both.

2   If a complainant does succeed before the tribunal, any award is charged to the LEA. It is not charged to the school budget unless it would be reasonable for the LEA to do so, and this is thought only to cover cases in which the governors have unreasonably defied LEA advice. For the governors, this of course means power with accountability but without penalty. For the LEA, it means picking up the bill for errors which they do not themselves effectively control.

3   Perhaps most significantly, the accountability structure is not compre-
     hensive. First, there are employment protection statutes omitted from
     the regime of governing body accountability to tribunals, and, second,
     the rules only apply to the exercise by governing bodies of four employ-
     ment powers, the powers conferred on them in relation to appointment,
     suspension discipline and dismissal by specific statutory provision.

This is not the place to consider in depth the more bizarre consequences
of these limitations. We can, for example, only wonder at how an aggrieved
teacher may seek legal redress against a decision of a governing body exercising its salary discretions with a taint of sex or race discrimination. Of
greater importance here is to demonstrate how the statutory framework is
constructed on a foundation which distinguishes quite different roles and
functions when dealing with under performing teachers.

Distinct roles and functions

The assumption, derived from the tradition, is that governing bodies hear
cases which headteachers present to them. The role of the governors is
almost judicial rather than managerial. They are not employers. The powers
they have are those conferred on them by Parliament. They do not include
powers of day-to-day personnel management. They have only the power to
make 'determinations' that a teacher employed to work at the school should
cease to work there. It is the power of determination of a 'case'.
    The 'case' they hear is that of the personnel manager, the headteacher. A
case which reaches a hearing before the first committee of the governing
body is a case defended, and any decision adverse to the teacher concerned
may be appealed to a second governors' committee. The system produces the
curious spectacle of a group of governors being invited by an experienced
advocate on behalf of the teacher to reject the judgement of the school's
senior manager.
    The adversarial pattern is one which is followed in the standard proce-
dures, and they are consistent with the statutes. The statutory regulations
insist that governing bodies cannot delegate their power to require the
removal of a teacher to an individual. It can only be delegated to committee.
There must be two committees, the first committee and an appeal
committee, each of at least three members; no governor may sit on both.
Again, the structure is designed to judge rather than manage.
    In standard procedures, once a decision has been made by the head that
measures designed to promote improvement in performance are not
succeeding, and formal procedures which may result in dismissal must
be invoked, the first committee is convened to conduct a hearing. The
first committee will be expected to listen to the head's report and
then hear the teacher's defence. Witnesses may be called, questioned and

cross-questioned. The order of submissions commonly follows the pattern of a civil trial.

The governors' appeal committee is convened at the initiative of a teacher who wishes to contest an adverse decision of the first committee. A decision to remove the teacher from the school, and so probably cause his or her dismissal, cannot be implemented until and unless endorsed by the appeal committee. A decision to dismiss (voluntary aided and foundation schools) or which causes dismissal (community and voluntary controlled schools) is implemented by giving notice due under the contract of employment. Summary dismissal is normally only possible in very serious misconduct cases. Because teachers' contracts are terminable by notice on only three days during the year – 31 December, 30 April or 31 August – the notice may be anything from two months to just under seven months.

Short of dismissal, the governors may issue warnings and final warnings. Apart from their disciplinary functions exercised in their statutory committees, they may also respond to underperformance by denying teachers whom they feel are under performing their normal experience point increase on the salary spine.

What the governors lack is the power to participate in the processes which may resolve problems of poor performance without the need for formal hearings. Again, the governing body's role in employment 'discipline' is to hear cases. They are not employers. They do not act as employers in the normal sense. They have quite specific statutory functions. They have employment powers; they do not have the powers of employers.

Foundation and voluntary aided schools

The governing bodies of these schools are employers in both the full and the normal sense. They take the role in personnel matters which they as governors think fit.

Promises

The system established in 1988 assumed for the headteacher the role of unit manager, both empowered and burdened with a range of managerial responsibilities which, in businesses of similar size, would be the function of three or four senior managers. The governing body became the equivalent of a policy-making board of directors, notionally overseeing expenditure decisions but in the main endorsing the decisions of the head or ratifying the inevitable. Much of the administrative support function formerly discharged by LEAs was diminished or removed.

In personnel matters, headteachers of county schools, deprived of ready access to professional support at senior level, became very lonely and potentially very vulnerable. They could not find comfort in their governing bodies because the governors lacked the necessary expertise and experience to give professional support, nor was it the statutory function of the governing body to intervene in personnel matters, particularly those involving professional judgement, other than in performing their 'hearing' role.

These problems for heads cut no ice of course with the last Conservative government. In the theoretical model for the education service, heads were senior managers and they should behave like senior managers without dependency on expensive public sector support teams. Governing bodies were there to be kept happy, in exchange for which they would give their support and encouragement. Otherwise the head must swim in the deep end, or sink.

In the spring of 1998, the new Labour government produced a draft code of practice to have effect under its new legislation redirecting the emphases in the education service. The legislation, the School Standards and Framework Act, restores to local education authorities a duty to raise and maintain standards within their areas. Though this legislation gives new names to traditional structures within the education service, in fact not a great deal is changed in structural terms. However, the redefinition of the LEA role, almost confined by the last government to that of an education funding agency, represents a cautiously expressed but fundamental change in philosophy. This is accompanied by a few changes in the law, the impact of which becomes clear only when they are put into their policy context. Chief Education Officers can, for example, ask the Secretary of State to direct governing bodies who wish to be assertively independent that they must listen to LEA advice on appointments and dismissals. CEOs will be legally entitled to make representations to the governing body on headteacher appointments and performance.

This pattern of minimal statutory change accompanied by large-scale policy changes within existing legal powers is becoming an increasingly apparent strategy of this government. At the time of writing the *Draft Code of Practice on LEA–School Relations* (DfEE 1998) begins to explain just such a change in education management policy. It devotes a long section to LEA influence and intervention in schools which the LEA may identify as giving cause for concern. While direct intervention is clearly seen as a reserve power to be used in extreme cases, LEAs are effectively being asked to restore to themselves many of the education management support functions which they abandoned after 1988. Now they are to be given the clear focus of raising standards.

The Code identifies that ensuring high levels of teaching performance is crucial to maintaining high standards. It acknowledges:

> While many governors may have experience of appointments, experi-
> ence of dismissal proceedings is much less common. Governing bodies
> should in all cases take great care to obtain high quality expert advice

and the LEA may be the best source of such advice. Consistent with the wider principles of this Code, the presumption should be that governing bodies should have discretion to make their own judgements. But if they misjudge, the LEA has powers to raise concerns and ultimately intervene if necessary.

This is encouraging language not heard within the education service for many years. It is unfortunate that it is negatively expressed in the context of dismissals, because the emphasis should be on aiding improvement to avoid dismissal, but the new sentiment is nevertheless encouraging. To believe that governing bodies could change to become the professional support for heads trying to deal with problems of under performance has really always been to believe in any port in a storm. The good role of governors is the quasi-judicial role with which they are familiar, though with the sense of desperation and adversarial antagonism removed. Professional teams making professional judgements should provide greater fairness for all involved, and certainly give heads that greater confidence in positive solutions which their vulnerability has so damaged.

And of course there is another factor. Headteachers also sometimes fail. If they experience difficulties, they too have the right to expect fair treatment, someone to help identify their problems and offer support through these problems. Their frustrated staff members would, no doubt, also like some active problem solving. As things have stood over the last ten years, there has been no one to do this. The Code of Practice plainly intends that this vacuum be filled.

Chapter 6

Governor involvement

This chapter will examine the role of the governing body in dealing with all poorly performing staff. The next chapter will deal specifically with the situation of a poorly performing headteacher, since in this case it will fall to the governing body to initiate proceedings against the head.

Introduction

Before 1988, the governing bodies of voluntary aided and special agreement schools were the employers of staff while for all other schools, which were state funded, the LEA was the employer. Under the 1988 Education Act, the governing bodies of LEA and voluntary controlled schools were given certain delegated employment powers and the governing bodies of the newly created grant-maintained schools became the employers of staff. For LEA schools, the governing body was given powers of appointment and dismissal, but any powers with regard to lack of capability of staff were less clear.

There is to be a redesignation of schools in April 1999. While individual governing bodies will have a small degree of negotiation, it is expected that schools will change as shown in Table 6.1. The role of any governing body has three aspects: responsibility for ensuring that

- legal procedures are followed
- the poor performer receives fair and ethical treatment
- the interests of children and other staff in the school are protected

Table 6.1 Employer status of school types before and after 1999

Pre-1999 designation	Post-1999 designation	Employer status
LEA maintained Voluntary controlled	Community	Quasi-employer
Grant-maintained	Foundation	Employer
Voluntary aided Special agreement	Aided	Employer

As the representative of employers, the governing body needs to ensure that the law is upheld. This particularly concerns employment and equal opportunity legislation, and more general rights of due process. The law must not only be followed, but be seen to be followed. This is important because, should an appeal be made to an industrial tribunal following dismissal, all details of the case will be scrutinised to ensure that procedures have been followed (see the example of Jim in Chapter 9). Related to this, the governing body has a moral duty to ensure that the poor performer is treated fairly and ethically. This involves ensuring that judgements and decisions are based on valid evidence and are made impartially. There should be a proper concern for the interests and well-being of the poor performer. However, these must be weighed against the interests of children and their education and the interests of other members of staff. The governing body is society's representative and is empowered to make judgements on these competing viewpoints.

The position of the governing bodies of aided and foundation schools is quite clear: they are employers and have the rights and duties of employers. The articles of government will have specified how far the headteacher has delegated powers of day-to-day management of staff. Consistent with these articles, the governing body should make clear how far it, or specified representatives, wishes to be involved in dealing with poor performers under capability procedures. Probably, reports to the chair of the staffing committee and/or the chair of governors will be required. As for other types of school, no one who has taken part in decisions at one stage of the process may be involved in any subsequent decisions to move for dismissal or to hear an appeal.

Specific requirements of LEA school governing bodies: community schools after 1999

The employer position of the governing bodies of community schools is more complex. It is clear that the governing body is required to set up a committee to ratify the decision of a headteacher to recommend a poor performer for dismissal when efforts to improve or move to an alternative post have failed. The committee either recommends dismissal or proposes an alternative course of action which may involve further remedial measures. In addition, an independent appeals committee may be needed if the member of staff appeals against the decision taken.

The instruments of government of schools in England currently allow the headteacher either to be a member of the governing body or to elect not to be a governor. However, except in the case where the poor performer is the headteacher, we do not consider that this makes a crucial difference to the relationship of the headteacher to the remainder of the governing body on matters of poor performance. The headteacher will have been delegated day-to-day control of the staff of the school, and so he or she should be the first to suspect and investigate possible poor performance. The only exception to this may be where a parental or other complaint has been made directly to the governing body. It is important if such an allegation is made publicly at a meeting of the governing body that this is speedily assigned to the head-teacher to investigate, and not discussed in detail at a full meeting of the governing body. This is because the governing body may need to set up the following committees under the revised capability procedures for teachers agreed in November 1997:

- Governors' Staffing First Committee
- Governors' Appeal Hearing

The members of both these committees must be able to judge the case impartially. This means they must have no prior involvement in the case. They may have prior knowledge of the allegation but not the findings of subsequent investigation nor any subsequent capability activities. These two committees must be independent of each other and may not share any members in common.

In order to prevent problems when the issue of poor performance first arises, it is important that the governing body adopts a policy on how it intends to deal with poor performance. This is best done in general terms and before the first case arises. Where the size of the governing body permits, some schools have standing committees to deal with all issues of capability, discipline and pupil exclusions.

Policy on poor performance

As this book continually emphasises, a good staff management policy is the best preventive measure to ensure that few staff if any need to be considered for capability procedures. So, in addition to setting up a policy on poor performance, the governing body might usefully check that a suitable organ-isational structure is in place such that each member of staff has a clear line manager who is responsible for monitoring their performance and taking action in the first instance when there is any first serious dip in performance. This should be supplemented with a clear staff appraisal and staff develop-ment policy.

The policy on poor performance should cover the informal and first formal stages of capability procedure for teachers in addition to the composi-tion and powers of the two formal committees suggested by the Revised Capability Procedures (RCP). The RCP only applies to teachers but the governing body should set up similar procedures for non-teaching staff in the school.

It is important that the size of these independent groups is considered, particularly for a governing body of a small primary school which may be quite small. The minimum number of members of each committee is three.

When cases start with suspected poor performance, it is probably wise for the headteacher not to mention any suspicions to any of the governing body until there is clear evidence of poor performance. Once informal actions to improve performance are proving insufficient and formal procedures are to start, then members of the governing body should be informed. This information should include the name of the teacher and that they are involved in capability procedures, but no further details lest this prejudice any decisions made by governors' committees should they be needed in the future. Such information should be given in confidence only to the governing body.

Teacher-governors will find themselves in a very difficult position. They are full members of the governing body and have a right to be fully involved in all actions of the governing body, but they probably will not wish to be directly involved in either of the formal committees. As they are bound by the same rules of confidentiality as other members of the governing body, they would be likely to find themselves in the very difficult position of being unable to discuss or justify any actions taken because of this. Their role should probably be to ensure that due process is carried out in a fair and ethical way.

Where members of the governing body receive complaints about teachers from parents or others, these should be reported to the headteacher for action rather than governors directly trying to deal with the situation. Such governors should not be involved in either of the formal governors' committees.

As has already been said, the governing body is legally responsible for its actions when exercising its employment powers. If it acts against professional advice or if it acts irresponsibly any costs which result may be charged against the school's budget, and if the member of staff takes action by bringing a case at an industrial tribunal, it is the governing body which would be required to defend its actions. Thus governing bodies are likely to be very cautious in taking action against poor performance.

Since 1996, OFSTED inspections have included reports initially on very good and very poor staff and, since 1997, all staff. Research evidence shows that such findings do not always accord with the expectations of the headteacher as to who among his or her staff is very good or very poor. For the purposes of this book, it is the reporting of very poor teachers which is the issue. There are cases where teachers receiving professional support have not been assessed as very poor teachers during inspection, and cases where OFSTED inspectors have reported poor teaching from staff who the headteacher did not consider to be performing poorly. It should be borne in mind that OFSTED inspectors visit a school for one week, and although their evidence base includes evidence other than observation of teaching when making their assessment, the circumstances in which they gather evidence are far from representative of day-by-day life in a school. Thus, evidence from OFSTED inspections should be treated as one piece of evidence but should not be taken to be definitive. However, where it corroborates suspicions of poor performance, it is likely to be a trigger for action.

Although the evidence from inspection is only one view of the performance of staff, it would probably be wise to investigate and gather further evidence if inspection raises the prospect of poor performance. The report of inspectors to the governing body and the published report will contain details of the inspection's findings, including its assessment of teaching performance. This will include statistics about the number of poor lessons – that is lessons graded less than 'satisfactory'. The headteacher will receive more detailed information. This can be used to allay fears of governors where the evidence of poor performance comes from the odd lesson from a number of staff rather than sustained poor performance from one or more members of staff.

Dealing with poor performance

Where poor performance has been substantiated and appears to be sufficiently serious to warrant steps which may lead to formal procedures for either dismissal or professional support, then appropriate governors should be informed pending report to a full governing body. This should only consist of the knowledge that a given individual is subject to capability procedures, with no details of the reasons lest this should prejudice any future decisions by the two formal governor committees.

If a first formal hearing before a governing panel becomes necessary, then the head must be able to produce evidence of poor performance and efforts to overcome this. Such evidence should involve judgements from others, particularly some persons independent of the school, to lessen any appearance that it is the judgement and conduct of the headteacher which is on trial. The headteacher must share all knowledge with this group. If the group are to take valid decisions, then they must be in possession of the relevant information. Although the group may rely on recommendations for action from the headteacher, they should have sufficient information so that they can judge appropriate action independently rather than only by proxy. A headteacher would be wise to ensure that evidence of poor performance is substantiated by other professionals, preferably including some from outside the school such as advisors or inspectors, so that there is no suggestion that the headteacher has any personal motives for his or her actions and that decisions on adequacy of performance are not solely dependent on his or her judgement.

The governors' hearing will need two kinds of assistance:

- legal/personnel advice
- independent professional judgement of performance

The school's LEA is likely to be involved in both. After poor performance has been substantiated and a preliminary assessment has been made about the severity of the case and expectations of improvement, the headteacher needs to contact the LEA as the formal employer of the poor performer (except for voluntary aided and foundation schools). The personnel section of the LEA should be able to give both legal advice and also good employment advice. They may want the poor performer to be seen by their representative, probably an LEA advisor or inspector, to confirm the poor performance.

As we have made clear, decisions to employ and dismiss staff are the prerogative of the governing body of a school. Representatives of the LEA, where it is the employer, may give advice and guidance to the governing body. It has a duty to consider any such advice and guidance; however, final decisions are the province of the governing body. This means that the governing body does not have to follow the advice or guidance. On the other hand, as we have also said, the governing body will be held accountable for its decisions and should have acted reasonably.

It would always be unreasonable to ignore advice, either legal or professional. The least that a governing body should do is to consider the advice or guidance. While the governing body need not follow such advice, it would be somewhat risky for lay people not to follow professional advice unless they had sought alternative professional advice. Needless to say, the alternative advice should be from equally eminent sources. The least that such advice should contain is that an alternative course of action would be as valid as that proposed by the LEA. If it were equally valid, the governing body would be entitled to take its own independent decision to suit its own circumstances following either course of action. Legal and professional advice and guidance is based on professional judgement, and may legitimately differ in its conclusions; thus the lay governing body should not accept such advice from its LEA as binding, but should feel free to take independent professional advice. This would either confirm the original advice or offer other possibilities.

Governing bodies should also beware of lay advice being offered by professionals. Where officers of the LEA or advisors are offering advice, governors should consider whether such advice has a professional basis or whether it is advice on which lay governors may have an equally valid opinion. If the advice does not rely upon specialist knowledge or experience but is merely sound common sense, then governors may be expected to have an equally valid opinion.

In the past there have been many occasions when headteachers or governing bodies have been dissuaded from action by LEA advice. While it is proper that unconsidered or illegal actions by a headteacher or governing body are prevented, there have been occasions where the timidity or reticence of LEA personnel has not been in the best interests of a school and has been based on opinion which has not been challenged. It is incumbent on a governing body to check advice which it does not believe to be sound or in the best interests of the school.

Such checking of advice could happen at any stage, since the governing body or the headteacher is likely to receive advice on a number of occasions. There will be initial advice about how to proceed, but further advice will be needed as actions progress. A particularly sensitive time is when there appears to be a stalemate. Typically this might involve the following:

- poor performance has been confirmed but is not very bad;
- some improvement has been made but this is disappointing and does not bode well for the future;
- the poor performer contests further action or appears to be unaffected by the process;
- the confirmed poor performer who is unable to improve shows no propensity to leave voluntarily.

Any decision about further action is likely to be finely balanced. There will be arguments which propose accepting the status quo in view of either the small degree of underperformance, or the great difficulties of securing any larger and long-lasting solution. Whether this is the appropriate course of action will depend upon individual school circumstances. Those in the school who are aware of the effects within the school of poor performance and its impact on the future are in the best position to balance the possibilities. Any assessment of future impact needs to weigh up the effect on the children influenced by the poor performer, and also the impact on other staff of a failure to achieve a satisfactory improvement in performance.

This is a particular case where, if the advice being given by the LEA does not accord with the needs of the school, an attempt should be made to ascertain how far such professional advice and guidance consists of opinions which are not shared by other equally qualified and experienced professionals.

As we have said before, not only does justice have to be done as regards employment legislation, but it has to be seen to be done. Thus, all meetings with the poor performer need to be recorded so that there is evidence, if it is required later, of what was done, by whom and when. Copies of all correspondence, from whatever source, need to be meticulously filed for future use.

Disciplinary procedure

Where poor performance results from a failure to perform which does not involve a lack of capability then disciplinary procedures are appropriate. They are also used for cases of misconduct and gross misconduct. For such a failure to perform, or for misconduct, the stages of the procedure are:

- oral warning
- written warning
- final written warning
- dismissal

For conduct so serious as to be deemed gross misconduct, such as putting children at risk, refusal to undertake contractual duties, or serious incapability through alcohol, the headteacher or governing body has the power directly to suspend the employee pending a full investigation. This may lead directly to dismissal by a properly constituted committee of the governing body. Any dismissed employee would have a right of appeal to an independent committee of the governing body.

Concluding comment

The governing body is in a pivotal position as regards poorly performing staff. It needs to be assured that the headteacher and his or her colleagues are taking action in cases of poor performance. Such expectations are made clear if the governing body sets up a clear policy on poor performance and how it should be dealt with. It has a formal role in confirming the suspension of a poor performer who has failed to improve and to recommend dismissal.

Chapter 7

Poorly performing headteachers and the role of the governing body

Introduction

Heads who are poor performers present a special case. They have no direct line manger and those whom they manage may be the ones who are most aware of the problem. Such heads also cannot be expected to be able to deal appropriately with any of their staff who are poor performers. Thus poor performance in headteachers, where it occurs, is an enormous problem. Throughout the remainder of this book we have assumed that the headteacher is the principal person dealing with poor performance of staff. When it is the headteacher who is not performing his or her job competently, a number of issues arise. The whole leadership of the school will be affected.

Diagnosing poor performance in the leadership of the school raises a whole series of problems. To begin with, the job of the headteacher is less closely prescribed than that of any other member of staff. Although there are certain functions which have to be carried out, the headteacher's job has a great deal of discretion. That discretion normally includes both setting the priorities of the job and also how it is carried out.

What is poor performance by a headteacher?

The job of the headteacher can be divided into:

* reactive maintenance aspects
* proactive developmental aspects

The first aspects are the ones most likely to be covered by a job description and the ones which are most likely to be noticed if they are not done or not done well. However, it is likely to be the more proactive elements which, if they are missing, will in the longer term be recognised as having handicapped the school in more subtle and more important ways.

The proactive elements of the job include those tasks which a good headteacher does which help to ensure the future success of the school: enhancing the reputation of the school, obtaining financial and other support; dealing with problems at a formative stage rather than when they have escalated into a crisis; and so on. If a poor headteacher does not do these sorts of tasks, it may be some time before the consequences are apparent.

The style in which the headteacher operates can vary from the highly autocratic to the highly democratic, and each can be successful in appropriate circumstances. Thus, any judgement of style needs to take account of the situation – and hence may be subject to differences of opinion – as well as legitimate differences in personal style.

All the causes of poor performance which have been described for other staff can apply to the headteacher. There may be a temporary problem due to either personal circumstances or events in school. Performance may have dropped off over a period of time, or the situation of the school may have changed and the head failed to respond. Finally, the performance of the head may be judged satisfactory in absolute terms but not be appropriate for the particular school in its particular situation with its staff and governing body.

While the causes of poor performance may be similar to those for other staff, the one crucial difference is that there is no one in a position to know about the head's poor performance and to do something about it in the same way that a headteacher would for any other member of staff. It follows from the above that it is likely to be the more reactive parts of the job where poor performance is most clearly likely to be apparent. However, this is most likely to be apparent to staff who are subordinate to the headteacher. Possibly deputy heads are in the best position to make an assessment of such failings. More junior staff may see only part of the picture and hence not be in a good position to know whether actions were appropriate given all the circumstances.

There are two ways of judging the performance of a headteacher:

1   outcomes
2   process

The first way of judging the head's performance is by what it achieves, or its outcomes. This should be reflected in the performance of a school. In its turn this raises two further questions. To what extent should the head be held accountable for performance and, secondly, how should performance be judged? The next section will deal with these issues.

The second way of judging a head's performance is by evaluating the processes by which the head carries out his or her work. First, this requires some framework to analyse the work of the headteacher, and, second, it requires an assessment of how well the headteacher performs on each aspect of the job profile. The second section below will pursue these issues.

Does poor school performance mean poor performance by the headteacher?

First, we shall discuss the difficulties of assessing the performance of a school before returning to the issues as to how far a headteacher should be responsible for school performance.

There are a number of criteria which could be used to assess the performance of a school:

1   output performance measures − for example, exam results, attendance and other published indicators;
2   progress or value added measures of children's progress;
3   OFSTED school inspection findings;
4   systematic satisfaction ratings from parents and pupils;
5   popularity of the school in terms of parental choice and reputation;
6   achievement of aims.

Each of these criteria has some difficulties. In the case of (1) there would need to be appropriate comparators so that the school's value on any indicator could be judged to be adequate or not. Deciding what are similar schools in order to perform a valid comparison is not easy. Having found valid comparisons, it is likely that the school will be adequate on some indicators and not on others. However, it is not only the level of the indicator as compared with similar schools which is important. A further factor to be considered is how these indicators are changing year by year. A school improving from a low base would probably be judged differently from a school declining from a high base.

Criterion (2) requires data on input scores of children when they enter the school and when they leave. If these are available, then it is possible to calculate whether the school is helping children make as much progress as other schools. Again, in addition to relative progress, there should also be a consideration as to whether progress is rising year by year or declining.

OFSTED school inspections judge a school on a wide range of performance measures but these are only carried out every six years for a typical school, although schools with weaknesses may be inspected more regularly. In addition to poor performance of the school, the inspection report is also likely to express a judgement on the leadership and management of the school.

Schools which have begun to collect systematic satisfaction ratings from parents and pupils have a further source of information with which to judge the performance of the school. A particular difficulty with this source of information is that there are no systematic comparative results from other schools, although there are some schemes operated by LEAs or universities which can give some comparative results using a specific instrument. In general, such measures of satisfaction could only be used as a means of indicating rising or declining trends over time as yearly statistics are built up by an individual school.

The popularity of a school can act as a crude barometer of parental approval, although any trends would need to take account of demographic data. Numbers on the school roll varying in proportion to the numbers of children of the appropriate age would indicate a neutral trend. Clearly this indicator is very crude, and may reflect all kinds of irrational decisions by parents. However, it is an indicator that a headteacher should be aware of, and to which they should react.

The achievement of aims is placed last not because it is least important, but because it is so difficult to assess unless a particular school has formulated its aims in a precise way that has led to progress being monitored by indicators which it has set up. Where a school believes that participation in after-school clubs, or sporting activities, or musical tuition or other activities, is important and has set up a valid means of assessing success at such activities, these would provide very important data for assessing the school's success. The lack of comparative data from other schools would still restrict any judgements to relative trends over time.

It should be clear that no one of these indicators alone should be taken as the measure of school performance. However, some combination of them could assess success across a wide range of activities. The precise weighting of such indicators for a particular school would need a good deal of discussion and should have been agreed well before the head's contribution to the achievement of these objectives comes under scrutiny. As governing bodies begin to agree performance targets with their headteachers, these need to include both remedial targets for correcting any current aspects of poor performance, and the more demanding developmental targets which may be connected with pay.

Having identified ways in which the performance of a school could be assessed, we move on to examine the contribution of the headteacher to the performance of the school. Although it is generally accepted that the headteacher makes a great deal of difference to the performance of a school, the situation is rather more complicated than the performance of the school being a direct reflection of the performance of the headteacher. As we indicated when we wrote about staff selection, a crucial element of the process is to identify a fit between the skills and attributes of the candidate and the needs of the post at a particular time in a particular school. A candidate may be a capable candidate in a generic sense but not for the particular job and its requirements. This is especially true of headship. A headteacher may have the qualities to lead another school in different circumstances but not to lead this school at this time. This situation, however, is rare and cases which are so bad as to be prominent are likely to involve fairly substantial omissions in terms of capabilities.

The lack of fit and capability is likely to show up more clearly in challenging circumstances. Schools in favourable circumstances and with capable staff are likely to provide a satisfactory performance under indifferent leadership. Over time, however, poor leadership will show up. On the other hand, a school with serious weaknesses will fail to respond successfully to anything but very good leadership, and leadership which is appropriate to those circumstances.

A similar 'level of competence' in leadership and management may have very different consequences in different circumstances. We envisage the 'challenging' circumstance as being where the school has been identified as having serious weaknesses or failings by OFSTED school inspections. These are often, but not invariably, schools in inner-city areas with high levels of social deprivation. These are areas where the job of teaching is much tougher than in areas where there is a more ready appreciation of the value of education and more support both financially and culturally, as shown in Table 7.1.

Areas of competence of headteachers

A number of attempts have been made to capture the job of the headteacher. The latest of these is the formulation by the Teacher Training Agency of a National Professional Qualification for Headship. This has lists of knowledge, skills and key areas of competence deemed necessary for a successful headteacher. However, that is very detailed and since it has not been validated by any research findings, its value in identifying poor performance is not known and it may not be suitable for use by a governing body.

The model proposed here is based on two aspects of headship identified by researchers some time ago. It has two principal dimensions, each of which have a number of components; these are presented in increasing order of proactivity. The two dimensions are 'leading professional' and 'chief executive'. The leading professional dimension covers those aspects of headship which explicitly require a professional educational background, while the

Table 7.1 The effect of school circumstances on quality of leadership

School circumstances	Leadership	Likely result
Challenging	Good	Improvement
	Weaknesses	Gradual worsening
	Poor	Rapid worsening
Favourable	Good	Improvement
	Weaknesses	Sporadic improvement
	Poor	Gradual worsening

chief executive dimension covers more generic leadership and management skills:

Leading professional
- teaching
- educational vision

Chief executive
- management
- relationships
- leadership

In each dimension, this ordering probably represents the order of difficulty in diagnosing and improving performance. This is not to suggest that it is easy to deal with poor teaching, but rather to suggest that it is more difficult to deal with the others since they also involve an effect on other adults.

Teaching

The procedures here are likely to be similar to assessing poor performance in other teachers with the exception that all judgements about poor performance will need to be made by outside professionals. Any starting point for judging performance should not be that the headteacher should be better than other teachers in the school. Headteachers should be chosen for their ability to lead and manage a school. They should be professionally competent as teachers but it is primarily as educators that they will lead and manage the education of children in school. They should not, however, be poor teachers. This becomes an absolute for a teaching head. In a small school where the headteacher is required to take a permanent teaching load, it might be thought that their performance standards should be similar to that for other teachers. However, there is an added complication; in addition to their teaching they are also required to carry out functions similar to those of headteachers of larger schools, but since they spend time teaching, they have less time to carry out similar management and leadership responsibilities. Research on teaching heads in small schools (Brock 1991, Morgan 1996) shows that the only way in which they can fit in all their work is by spending less time than they would like on some aspects of the job; often this means preparation and marking. They are generally still able to teach at least satisfactorily because they are experienced and good practitioners. It would probably be wise for appointing bodies for teaching heads to ensure that the latter have a higher teaching competence than might be required of other headteachers, so that even when they are forced to spend less time on preparing their teaching they will still be likely to deliver an acceptable performance.

Educator

Heads of larger schools are likely to be able to choose the extent and nature of their teaching, and thus it is more likely to be their skills as educators which are more critical than their ability as teachers. Heads are required to have a base of knowledge and expertise about how children should be educated. This is not the same as their being able to teach. As heads, they are required to take an overview of all that goes on in a school. They need to be able to diagnose what is needed, and ensure that they and their teachers deliver it. They need to keep abreast of educational developments and have ideas about worthwhile innovations and improvements which could be introduced at an appropriate stage. Although others in schools can contribute to these and may be a source of ideas, the head is expected to be the leading professional advisor to the governing body and be capable of offering advice both about external requirements which the school is expected to meet, and about the priority which should be given to internally generated improvements.

Management

The foregoing provides the professional base on which the head manages a school. The headteacher needs to ensure that there are systems in place for:

- curriculum development and monitoring
- staff management
- financial management
- external relations

It is probably in the area of financial management, and particularly the more routine aspects of budgetary information and control, where governors are likely to be aware of any shortcomings. While the other areas are likely to require professional judgement, governors should be able to judge the extent to which planning is based on information, the implementation of plans is monitored, and activities are systematically monitored and evaluated. Warning signs are likely to be a lack of administrative systems, frequent crises, paucity of factual information, and frequent unplanned reactions to events.

The headteacher needs to be capable of taking an overview of all the operations in a school and appreciating the inter-relationships between the different aspects. This, and an appreciation of longer-term progress, is at the heart of strategy. There should be processes in operation which demonstrate that any strategy is soundly based.

Relationships

Management and leadership rely upon a relationship with children, parents, staff and governors. There are also relationships with the community, LEA, and so on. At the heart of many relationship problems is communication, either currently or in the past. The need to explain and provide information is fundamental to good management. Where there is poor communication, people are left to make their own surmises about what is happening and why. This may lead to mistrust and provide a fertile breeding ground for those with imagination.

From time to time, there will be genuine differences of opinion which spring from deep-seated differences of values between individuals. Often the differences between such values are implicit rather than being made explicit. The apparent differences are about opinions and priorities, and where there does not seem to be respect for the other person's point of view. Relationships are unlikely to be repaired if respect, honesty and shared confidence are lacking. These are difficult issues because there are at least two parties involved, and both need to co-operate for good working relationships.

A particular relationship of which the governing body will have first-hand experience is the relationship of the headteacher with the governing body. If the headteacher fails to recognise the policy-making role of the governing body, or fails to act on policies set by the governing body, or fails to provide information requested by the governors, the governing body may decide that this is an aspect of the headteacher's performance which it cannot tolerate.

Leadership

Finally, there is that indefinable quality, leadership. Leadership is only demonstrated by 'followership'; therefore, if the headteacher has little impact on staff and pupils, there can be no leadership. There are many forms of leadership other than the heroic 'Arnold of Rugby' model, but all need to have the effect of causing others to move forward and have confidence that the school is in good hands. Where there are administrative systems in place which work and the routine aspects of management appear to be taking place, any failure to bring about improvement in a school must involve some failure of leadership. This may be a failure to diagnose a need for movement or an inability to lead the improvement. The leader needs to convince others of the importance of the school's work and help them recognise a value and meaning to their activities. He or she needs to recognise and share a need for change and improvement and to convince others that he or she has a strategy for the future of the school. Good leaders delegate, but the leadership of the whole school cannot be delegated: this is the task of the headteacher.

How should poor performance be tackled?

There are two basic stances which the governing body can take to the performance of the headteacher:

1 proactive
2 reactive

In (1), if the governing body has suspicions that the headteacher is a poor performer then it, and this usually means the chair of governors, can seek information from the LEA about its professional assessment of the performance of the headteacher. Depending on what such a request yields, the governing body could ask the LEA to investigate and to implement capability procedures for the headteacher if necessary.

In (2), the governing body waits for complaints from staff or parents or an approach from the LEA intimating that there are professional worries about the competence of the headteacher. By this stage it would be clear that an investigation of performance was necessary and that this might lead to capability procedures.

In addition to these two basic stances of the governing body, there are also two possible types of poor performance for established headteachers: temporary and long-standing. Thus there are four possibilities of action. Table 7.2 below suggests a course of action in each case.

Table 7.2 Governing body approaches to temporary and long-standing poor performance

	Stance of governing body	
Length of poor performance	Reactive	Proactive
Temporary	(a) Wait for the issue to be raised by the head or eventually raise it with the head as things get worse	(b) Raise the matter with the head and, if appropriate, agree challenging targets and monitor progress
Long-standing	(c) Wait for OFSTED report, approach from LEA or complaints	(d) Approach head/LEA

Reaction to temporary poor performance

Where there has been previous good performance from a headteacher, it may be a little time before the signs are noticed that the school is running less well than it did. There may be more incidents, a lack of follow-up action to governors' comments, parental complaints, and so on. Depending on the relationship of the chair of governors to the head and the predisposition of the chair of governors, it may be appropriate for the chair to raise the matter with the head in a personal interview, if the matter has not already been raised by the head. The alternative is to seek help from the LEA. The following case study illustrates an example.

Don had been head for seven years. He had been appointed at the age of 44 and had thrown himself wholeheartedly into his new role. He had been instrumental in turning a mediocre secondary school into a popular and lively place with good examination results and a committed staff. However, over the last year, governors had gradually become aware that little action was taking place as a result of decisions made. Day-to-day management of the school seemed to be more lax, Don was seen around the school less and less frequently and much of the management of the school seemed to have been gradually delegated to the two deputy heads. There was, as yet, no concrete evidence of poor performance, but it seemed that it would not be long before problems would arise. The chair of governors decided to investigate: it turned out that Don was thoroughly bored. He felt that he had done all he could to improve the school and that his role of now maintaining the high standards set was predominantly a more passive one than the one he had been appointed to: the job had substantially changed. There was no simple answer to this. At 51, Don could not be sure of successfully applying for a second headship, but he could still have nine years in his present post.

This case illustrates the importance of context in performance. Heads (and others) have particular skills and propensities. Some are good at turning a school around while others are good at the more long-term process of further improving an already good school. The appointment of heads on indefinite contracts inhibits movement that might allow heads to move on when they have accomplished the change in the school for which they were appointed and which suited their talents.

Proactive stance to prevent poor performance

A headteacher does not have a clear line manager who could take the role of diagnosing potential poor performance as would be the case for other staff. There may be a liaison officer in the LEA who takes a pastoral role with respect to a number of schools, but the main person to whom a head can relate when assessing the performance of the school is the chair of governors. Thus there is preventive action which the governing body can take, which is to set challenging targets for the head and monitor progress towards the targets. Such targets could be for both the school and for the personal development of the headteacher.

Reaction to long-term poor performance of a headteacher

A governing body which takes a reactive stance waits for evidence of poor performance to be brought to its attention. This can be in the form of staff or parental complaints, the results of an OFSTED school inspection, or through an LEA officer bringing some professional concerns to the governors' attention. It falls to the governing body to initiate any investigations and to take further decisions following investigation. The governing body must do one of two things: either ask the LEA to investigate with a view to providing the headteacher with competency support procedures if there is substantiation of poor performance; or, after investigation, decide that the existing evidence and suspicions did not warrant such action.

Case study: LEA intervention

Janice was the head of a junior school in her mid-fifties. She had been head at this school for almost twenty years. There had been occasional concerns about her drinking in the past, but it was the poor progress of the school in raising achievement which led the LEA to encourage the governing body to look more critically at Janice's performance. The governors recognised a possible connection between the number of parental complaints and the head's performance, and asked the LEA to investigate. A senior officer who had been a head and was an OFSTED inspector acted as investigating officer. He advised the governors that there was a problem and that they could either proceed with a disciplinary procedure or with a case of incapacity. The head went off sick. *What should the governors do?*

Case study: OFSTED inspection evidence

Mark had been head of a secondary school for twelve years. Everyone said that he was a very nice person and was very fond of him, so rarely pressed any issues which might have been confrontational. The most clear evidence of indecision in the school was a growing budget problem. There was an unexpected deficit at the end of the year, and worse to come the year after. An OFSTED inspection produced a fairly poor report which criticised standards in a number of areas and cited lack of positive leadership. At this juncture the governors took the initiative and persuaded the head to leave before formal procedures were implemented.

Proactive stance in the case of long-standing poor performance

A recent further source of unsolicited evidence on the performance of the headteacher is an OFSTED inspection report. If this contains any criticism of the leadership and management of the school, then this will require an action plan to deal with it. This would trigger professional advice from the LEA. In the cases below, either the governing body took the initiative to have the suspected poor performance investigated formally, or the governing body pursued the issue after receiving inspection evidence.

Case study: proactivity by the governing body

Harold was the established head of a secondary school in a pleasant suburban area. The school was not doing badly but it had persistent weaknesses which were glossed over each year. The chair of governors was the local vicar although this was not a church school. He was very easy-going and charitable. He did not recognise pressures building up among parents and governors about the disappointing examination results. However, newly elected governors proposed a new chair who was elected. He was a powerful local political figure who was determined that there should be changes. The head was immediately put under pressure and within a few months had accepted voluntary early retirement.

Case study: proactivity following an OFSTED report

Thomas had been the head of an inner-city church primary school for twelve years. An OFSTED inspection identified the school as requiring special measures as there was low achievement and inconsistency in teaching standards. Leadership in the school was perceived as good in setting moral standards but poor in curricular issues. The report led to anger in the governing body, who considered that they had been misled by the head about standards in the school. A new chair was appointed who had experience as a governor of another inspected school. She was determined that the issues be properly addressed. Concerns intensified when the head appeared to play little part in devising the action plan in the school and left it to the deputy. The new chair of governors put pressure on the head to deliver the action plan and kept asking for information. She consulted the diocesan board and the LEA about her concerns. The consensus was that the school would not move forward under the present headteacher, and the headteacher was beginning to show signs of stress. A package was devised by the LEA and offered. The LEA and the diocesan director both met with the head and explained the consequences if the action plan did not work. The head with some reluctance took early retirement. He felt 'pushed out', but realised that he was being asked to perform at a level which he could not meet.

In this second case, it may be considered that the governors took a rather pre-emptory decision about the capabilities of the headteacher after taking advice. While the full picture would be needed to judge the reasonableness of the governors' actions, the position of the headteacher is a very special one. It more than any other reflects on the school. Thus a protracted period of support for a head in a school which is in a vulnerable position has particular repercussions for the education of children in the school.

Headteachers have the same employment rights as other staff. They can expect similar assistance in improving any poor performance if they wish to remain in post. They may leave their post without such attempts to improve by negotiation and with their agreement. Any such termination of their contract without either their agreement or after appropriate assistance to improve would leave the governing body open to an allegation of unfair dismissal, which could be pursued by the head at an industrial tribunal.

Others who may become involved

Who are others who may be in a position to do something about poor performance of headteachers? When appraisal for headteachers was first being considered, it was clear that they were in an anomalous position in not having the equivalent of a line manager. If there was a supervisory education officer or link advisor, their position as a line manager became more ambiguous following the 1988 Education Act than it was before, since they do not appoint staff in schools nor dismiss them. However, these may be highly influential players in any actions to diagnose and improve poor performance of headteachers.

Following the Education Reform Act of 1988, it is the governing body of all schools which has the power to appoint and dismiss staff. Thus it is the chair of governors and, to a lesser extent, the remainder of the governing body who are key players. Having identified the chair of governors as a crucial influence, some difficulties follow. The chair may spend only a little time in school and sometimes may only regard his or her role as a ceremonial one. He or she may be highly reliant on the headteacher for knowledge of what to do. In any case, chairs are likely to have a close relationship with the head and may feel a proprietary sense of support for the headteacher. Any evidence of poor performance may be difficult to independently assess if the chair is heavily dependent on the head for information about the school and its personnel.

Any discussion of the performance of the headteacher at the governing body or its committees will leave staff representatives in a very difficult position. They may not wish to be disloyal to the head, or they may fear for their future career if the head regards them as untrustworthy.

It is likely to be one or more issues coming up in the normal course of events which appears to cast doubts on the competence of the head and may provoke some informal comments amongst the governing body. These may often involve differences of opinion, and it may be difficult to decide whether there are serious problems. Any individual incident is likely to be dismissed as an isolated case, and it may be some time before a pattern is noticed. It is only at the stage when a potential pattern has been recognised that any further steps can be contemplated.

Although a governing body will almost certainly need professional educational advice about the performance of the headteacher, governors are now in a much better position to know about the performance of a school than previously. There are well publicised examination results which allow national and local comparisons. Most LEAs now publish comparative data on a whole range of factors, both outcome and process factors, which provide some comparisons with other similar schools. Finally, there is information from school inspections carried out under the OFSTED framework. It is this latter source which has both provided systematic evidence on the performance and management of a school and has also been the trigger for the poor performance of headteachers to be tackled.

Research evidence shows that many headteachers resign in the run-up to an OFSTED inspection, and a number leave shortly afterwards. Not all of these departures represent poor performance, but there is evidence that often this is the case. Follow-up of failing schools shows that half of such schools have a new headteacher as part of the improvement of the school. The source of pressure appears to be a recognition of poor performance in the preparations for inspection, either by the head or by advisors and others helping the school prepare. In some cases, it is the recognition of their responsibilities by governors which causes them to question the performance of the headteacher when questions are asked about the performance of the school in the run-up to inspection.

Poor leadership and management may be described in the inspection report, and this may be a key issue for action following inspection. If this is the case, poor performance will have been highlighted and be formally on the agenda. Governors are required to produce an action plan which responds to such key issues. Unlike other points for action, where the headteacher is likely to be an important input into the action plan, here governors have to take the initiative. The verbal feedback session by inspectors to the governing body is likely to be a very important occasion. Inspectors should be asked for the evidence on which they have based their judgement of poor leadership and management. These should provide a factual basis for any further investigation into alleged poor performance.

The *Draft Code of Practice on LEA–School Relations* (DfEE 1998) gives the LEA a duty to raise matters of poor performance of the headteacher with the governing body of all schools: LEA, foundation and aided. This is intended to be done informally at first, and then as an official report requiring a response if informal actions do not achieve results.

The governing body in all cases will need professional advice both about the performance of the head and about how to proceed. A governing body which acts precipitately or does not follow appropriate procedures may find itself having to defend its action before an industrial tribunal if it is accused of unfair dismissal.

In principle, the course of action is similar to poor performance of other staff:

- investigate
- agree a course of action
- monitor progress and take appropriate further steps if progress is inadequate

However, while the steps may be similar, the repercussions are not. Poor leadership from the head will affect the whole school and, if action follows an OFSTED inspection report, events will be more public than for other staff. This is a time when great damage can be done to the school in the eyes of parents and potential parents. Thus, any action to investigate and remediate substantiated claims of poor leadership and management should be progressed as fast as reasonably possible without prejudicing such remediation.

A governing body would not be in a position to carry out these steps unaided and would probably use an advisor or inspector from the LEA to carry out the investigation since, inevitably, professional judgements will be required in order to substantiate or not charges of poor performance. Other forms of such expertise are the diocesan boards for church schools. Discussing the evidence with the head and agreeing a course of action and some precise targets will also require professional knowledge. Finally, assessing how far progress, following remedial measures, is appropriate in the circumstances will need professional judgement. A governing body will require such actions to be carried out on its behalf and will wish to hear the result. This should be reported to the Governors' Staffing First Committee. This will either complete the matter if improvement has taken place, or proceed to a recommendation of dismissal if not.

All of this will be at its most difficult when the cause of poor performance concerns style of leadership or the more proactive aspects of leadership. In both these cases, perception and confidence will be important considerations and these are difficult to assess. They are also difficult to improve, since they flow from personal characteristics of the head rather than simple new procedures to be learned, which might be the case in the more mechanical aspects of school management.

Lately there have been cases where the governing body has come to the conclusion that it is unable to continue to work with the headteacher. This may be due to a lack of trust or to serious differences of opinion between influential governors and the headteacher. Where relationships have broken down, something has to happen in the best interests of the school. In the worst case, from the head's point of view, he or she may not be incompetent but just unable to work with that particular governing body. The governing body needs to have confidence in the headteacher, and it is difficult to see an ideal course of action where trust breaks down in a fairly fundamental way. Either the governing body must change or the headteacher must go. Whatever the moral arguments, the governing body has the formal power to take steps to remove the headteacher.

Concluding comment

Where it is the headteacher who is suspected of performing poorly, it is the governing body who should initiate action. This requires that it has information on the performance of the school and of its head. The governing body should call on LEA professional advice if they have reasonable suspicions that the headteacher is not performing adequately. In any case, it should respond to complaints and see that these are properly investigated.

Part II

Chapter 8

Particular groups and issues

Introduction

This chapter examines the issues involved in poor performance for five particular groups of teaching and non-teaching staff. It discusses the issues and illustrates them with a number of actual cases. These cases vary in length so as to illustrate fundamental features of the example. The chapter is divided up into the following subsections.

- temporary problems
- new staff
- established staff
- middle managers (including deputy headteachers)
- support staff

There are obviously many ways in which these categories overlap and other categories could have been chosen, but these headings seemed best to help pinpoint issues of a specific nature or that are particularly relevant to a member of staff's length and quality of experience or their role within a school or college. Comments made or cases referred to in any one section could often have sat equally comfortably in a different section. Where appropriate, cross references are made.

As we have stated earlier in this book, poor performance is not limited to one particular group in education, nor to a particular moment in a career cycle. There is no limit to its causes: each individual can perform at an unsatisfactory standard because of any combination of different professional and personal factors. It might be the result of management decisions or policies, incompatibility of personalities, ineffective recruitment strategies, a mismatch of skills to the job, innovation fatigue or any of the external pressures felt by people living in today's complex society. The problem might be as fundamental as a wrong choice of career — there are some people whose skills are not suited to a career in education — or a wrong choice of school — different types of school have different cultures and different expectations of both their staff and their pupils. In these cases, the solution to the problem is probably less straightforward than the cause. Qualifications (insufficient for direct movement into another career or only suitable for teaching) or a financial or personal situation might make it difficult for someone to move out of the sector or into different schools.

Sometimes it is difficult to assess objectively what constitutes poor performance. Poor management decisions may cause poor performance in the classroom. The latter is comparatively easy to identify and evidence is often easily obtained through observation. The cause, however, might not be the classroom teacher but the subject co-ordinator or the senior manager insisting on the use of a particular teaching strategy or assessment that might not be appropriate to the subject or the pupils. Poor performance might be the result of management decisions about recruitment, staff development, resourcing, and so on. Cause and effect are rarely as directly related as they might seem at first glance. This section explores some of these issues through actual cases.

Recognition of poor performance is sometimes very clear: missed deadlines for assessments, unmarked books or recurring disruption in classes are unmistakable signs that a problem exists and can be used immediately as the basis for investigation of that problem. More often, it is less easy to point immediately to evidence. It may start off with a line manager having a feeling that the atmosphere in a classroom does not feel quite right. It may be that the number of days' absence of a particular member of staff seems to be increasing for no obvious reason. It may be a change in someone's behaviour or a chance remark at a parents' evening. If, as must always be the preferred option, performance is to be improved with the least detrimental effect on pupils' progress and staff morale (the morale of either the underperforming member of staff or more widely), then remedial action taken early is more likely to be successful than a more formal approach when evidence has built up into a more concrete form. In a school where senior managers work very closely with staff in a culture that encourages improvement in a non-punitive but developmental and open manner, it is more likely that signs of potentially poor performance can be picked up and acted on at a very early stage. In a closed or defensive atmosphere, poor performance can be hidden until it becomes a problem that is difficult to resolve without harming aspects of the work of the school.

It goes without saying that staff who feel confident about themselves and their work are less likely to underperform. They are not necessarily more competent by nature, but are more likely to support each other in working to high standards and to ask for help when a problem occurs. Much underperformance is avoided by good managers dealing effectively with isolated incidents before these can become a pattern that then becomes difficult to break.

Temporary problems

Staff who are normally competent may experience periods in their professional lives where they are not able to function to the standard expected either by their peers or by their managers. The knowledge that they are not meeting their own standards may exacerbate their failure because they may lose self-confidence and, at the same time, use inappropriate strategies to try to cover up their problems. If the reason for the dip in performance is understood by those in a position to give support, the latter can then adopt appropriate strategies to remedy the situation and to avoid any long-term effects on either the member of staff or the pupils who are influenced by their work. The ability to overcome this dip will be dependent on several factors, including the individual's resilience, stamina and motivation, the management style of the school's leaders and the quality and timeliness of INSET opportunities.

Change in the requirements of the job

Temporary problems could be caused by a change in the requirements of the job. There have been so many changes in every area of education in the last decade that it is likely that the vast majority of people involved in work in schools have, however briefly, experienced a feeling of being unable to cope with the demands made on them. Teaching staff have had to deal with fundamental changes to the curriculum. In some areas this has resulted in substantial deskilling: subject areas (such as science, geography and maths) have been redefined to include topics previously accepted as part of different subjects and which were probably not part of the degree course studied by the teacher. New skills and knowledge have had to be acquired and then immediately applied in the classroom.

The following scenario is typical of the experience of many teachers in both primary and secondary schools. These are the classroom teachers who have formed the backbone of the profession with their conscientiousness and stability. They are not high-fliers but dedicated to working with the pupils in their care. It is this group that has probably been most affected by the seemingly unabated flow of changes in education.

Doreen

Doreen had been teaching maths in a high school all her career. She had been college trained, seeing no reason to study at university when she knew that she wanted to be a teacher and nothing else. She had never aspired to being a head of department, but was gratified when offered the responsibility of being second in department in recognition of her assiduous work over the years. Not one to make changes at a whim, she had gradually developed her methods and materials until she was totally satisfied with them. Her pupils were achieving pleasing results at 'O' level and in CSEs. Then came the GCSE. She was convinced that she could not change her methods to adapt to this new examination but, working with a head of department who knew her well, and was confident that she had the ability to make the necessary changes, she slowly made the transition and began to feel confident again. Her pupils continued to be successful. When the National Curriculum was imposed, Doreen was ten years older, and a new head-teacher and head of department were in post. The school was also having a new teaching block built to replace 'temporary' classrooms put in place when the school leaving age was raised to 16. Doreen had always taught in one of these classrooms. She once again, and more deeply this time, felt that she could not make the necessary changes, so refused to exchange the room in which she had always worked for one in the new block. This time it seemed to the head of department that she used her unwillingness to change rooms as a strategy to avoid facing her fear of the curriculum changes. As the move became imminent she became ill. Eventually she was persuaded to move to a new room and to join the rest of the department in INSET. It was only when she realised that it was a learning experience for everyone concerned that her fear receded and she began to adapt herself to the new requirements. (In the end she was only partly successful and took the opportunity of early retirement the following year.)

It is often difficult for senior managers to understand the motivation of conscientious classroom teachers who enjoy the confidence gained from a thorough knowledge of their subject or age range and the materials they use. Such teachers take no pleasure in what they see as change for change's sake and feel that they are not doing their best for their pupils when they no longer feel totally at ease with the materials they have been using. Consequently, they feel a return of the lack of confidence that they thought had disappeared with the end of their probationary year. They also feel excluded from any decisions about the implementation of change. It is particularly when people feel helpless that they are most likely to lose the motivation necessary to carry them through the period of change. Good managers will try to avoid this by involving staff as much as possible in managing the changes, agreeing together what has to be implemented as it stands and where they can work together to adapt new requirements to suit their own school or college needs. Where involvement is not possible, staff will at least be kept informed of planned changes and their implementation timetable. It has been difficult for managers to assess the speed of change. They have wanted to implement changes as quickly as possible (an OFSTED inspection might be imminent) but have had to be sensitive to the ability of staff to assimilate new concepts and the time needed to move from assimilation to implementation. This relies on the skills of individual managers to know when to lead by inspiring confidence in their knowledge of the way forward and when to lead by involving others in a common learning experience.

Similarly fundamental, and probably even more difficult to assimilate, have been the changes in methods of assessment. An otherwise highly competent teacher of a Year 6 class totally misunderstood what was required by the assessment documentation for Key Stage 2 English and was mortified at what she perceived to be 'letting down the pupils' when her assessments did not comply with requirements. This was not helped by the deputy head's impatient reaction caused by his own anxiety about collating the information accurately and in time for a deadline imposed externally. Whatever is new causes concern to everyone involved. It seems that where anxieties are shared, there is less likelihood of performance being below expectations for any length of time. Where individuals are struggling on their own they are more likely to risk failure, however temporary.

The job has not changed but the people have

Sometimes the job itself has not changed but fellow workers have, so the individual remaining from the original group suddenly finds that the established way of doing things is not automatically accepted by the new group. Confidence is shaken and a period of nervousness results in visibly poor performance. There are several ways in which such a scenario can come about. The most frequently occurring is when a year head or co-ordinator takes responsibility for a different year group but the teachers or tutors in that year remain the same (see the example of Jane in Chapter 9). Different leaders have different styles, as can be seen from attendance at assemblies led by different year co-ordinators. One may have a much more informal style than another, encouraging pupils to respond and interact, while another believes that there should be an atmosphere of reverential silence. In leading the relevant groups of staff, co-ordinators will probably also show substantial differences in expectations. Success will depend on the attitude of the rest of the group and the willingness of everybody to adapt. The co-ordinator has the same outcomes in mind as when working with a different year group, but will probably have to adopt different strategies in order to achieve success with the new group. It is always more difficult to manage change with an established group than with a newly formed one.

The established group is likely to see no reason to change, has worked successfully together already, and is probably a good example of a mature team. The group feels no ill will towards the new leader but genuinely sees no reason to change its way of working. This can substantially undermine the confidence of a new leader, especially if they find what they perceive as persistent stonewalling by the group. The work of the group is then not seen to be progressing and the leader is seen to be failing.

If the senior managers had been able to foresee this problem they could perhaps have been able to make other changes to the year groups, where possible, to create a new team for the new leader to develop. If this is not possible, the new leader could have a brief to implement a specific change linked to known expertise. This would enable them to have an opportunity to make successful changes and the group can share in the success, thus creating a perception that the new team is a successful one. Creating a situation in which the leader is not successful eventually leads to poorer performance throughout the group while they are not working towards the same goals. It is therefore crucial to avoid such a situation if at all possible.

A similar situation to the above could arise when a series of staff departures changes the nature of the working group although the leader remains the same. The leader does not foresee that the culture of the group will change (perhaps changing from a mature team to one that needs to restate its working framework) and does not use appropriate strategies for leading the new team.

Individual, personal problems

However professional people try to be, there are times when circumstances in their personal life have an effect on their performance. These circumstances can involve relationships, family or health problems.

Roberta

Roberta had regularly taken recreational drugs as a student. When she moved to a different town to start work as a college librarian she had made a new group of friends who were not into drugs and she left behind her student behaviours. She enjoyed her work and soon developed a close friendship with one of the lecturers, James. This relationship deepened over the next two years and they set up home together. Roberta's line manager was sufficiently pleased with her work to suggest her as project leader for some research commissioned by the college and due to start the following September.

Just before the end of the summer term James applied for and was successful in obtaining a post in New Zealand, a three-year contract starting in the autumn. Roberta and James spent the summer together but started the new college year apart. At first Roberta was motivated by leading the project but gradually other members of the working party began to complain about lack of direction and poor communication. Her line manager kept an eye on her progress, anxious that her protégé should succeed. She had a personal stake in Roberta's success as it was she who had put her name forward to lead the project, but perhaps she had persuaded Roberta to take on a task that was beyond her ability at this early stage in her career.

Understandably, she was looking for a professional explanation for Roberta's poor performance. In fact, Roberta had heard from James that he had found another girlfriend in New Zealand and she was so devastated that she had taken refuge in her old habits, not during the week but at weekends, and in her feelings of rejection had cut herself off from her local friends. It was only when a concerned colleague made a chance remark that Roberta broke down and allowed her feelings to be known. From here it was possible to begin to help her. She took some time off while she sought medical and psychological advice, and was supported through this by colleagues who soon became friends. This created a supportive structure for her to recover her self-esteem and to return to her work at the beginning of the new year.

This case raises many issues, moral and legal as well as of capability, but it figures here as a reminder that relationships (intimate and social) naturally take precedence over the demands made by paid employment and it would be inhuman to ignore this. Roberta was, and is, very good at her work, and by supporting her through a period of personal trauma, the college retained an excellent librarian.

Another usually highly competent teacher was experiencing a lot of difficulties with his two teenage children while his wife was working abroad. One had recently started a university course and was finding it difficult to settle in to university life, while the other was spending far too much time, according to his parents, drinking with his friends and not getting on with his work. The teacher felt that he was failing to ensure they worked as they would if their mother had been there and he was beginning to fall into the vicious circle of criticism and disagreements that can be typical of parents' relationships with teenagers. His unhappiness and sense of failure with his own children began to be replicated in his feelings towards the pupils he taught and his teaching became less effective. His wife's return and their elder child's success in coming to terms with life at university helped him return to his normal standard of work, but it is easy to see how the situation could have needed someone in school to help support the father while the problem was there. There are many members of staff who are single parents and, without being paternalistic, those in management positions need to be aware of the pressures and difficulties likely to be experienced.

Medical conditions

Sometimes medical conditions can contribute to poor performance. This can be a particularly difficult problem as the people concerned probably do not know what is happening, other than being aware that they are less effective than they ought to be in their work. The medical condition could be a newly developing one and a source of great anxiety to the sufferer, or it could be a chronic condition gradually affecting the person's ability to function at a high level. Whatever the cause, it is often difficult for those responsible for the member of staff's work to weigh the relative short-term and long-term needs of the teacher against those of the pupils. It never has been acceptable for anyone to continue to perform at an unsatisfactory level over an extended period of time. Currently, heavy pressure is exerted on managers to deal promptly with poor performance, but changes in procedures have resulted in retirement on grounds of ill health being less easy to achieve than it has been in the past.

There are many examples where retirement on grounds of ill health has been used as a way of removing a member of staff whose work has been unsatisfactory (see the example of George in Chapter 9). Very often, difficulties with carrying out functions in school lead to periods of absence with stress-related illnesses. Retirement has been a successful strategy in that it has avoided extended capability procedures and has enabled the person concerned to leave the school or college concerned without loss of dignity. It has avoided a great deal of unpleasantness, but it is now less likely to be used in this way as it becomes more and more difficult to obtain early retirement on any grounds.

Martin

In Martin's file was a copy of a reference written by a previous head of his school for a post he applied for in April 1980. The following is an adapted extract from this:

> Since Sept. 1976 he has been in charge of resources. The reason that prompted me to move Mr Daws from technology teaching to resources was that he was failing as a teacher of children but had considerable organising ability and was happier with his head inside a television set...

Martin came to the school as a newly qualified teacher of technology, so was exempt from probation. From the beginning he seems not to have achieved success as a teacher, but there is no evidence of any action being taken other than the attempt to minimise his influence by changing his role as mentioned above. He seemed to be aware of the problems that he was having but covered them by getting children to work in small groups elsewhere in the school; for example, in the library, computer room, and so on. He regularly complained that management decisions prevented him from carrying out work effectively. The head of department tried to give him classes where he would cause the least trouble.

A new headteacher came to the school in 1990.

The medical situation started in November 1992 with a leg pain which continued over a whole year. The situation was made more difficult because Martin was known personally by many people in the locality: for example, he belonged to a local church choir and the historical society.

The school governors agreed to extend his period on half-pay for an additional term because of his long connection with the school and the community. He didn't seem to want early retirement on grounds of ill health, and returned to school in April 1994. Discipline problems soon recurred. The headteacher started capability procedures at the same time as the problem of his continuing poor state of health was being discussed. The head of department wrote to the head stating her concerns about the quality of his teaching and her discussions with Martin about strategies to improve classroom discipline and particularly safety in the workshops. At one point a pupil was seen hanging upside down out of a window (fortunately the workshops are on the ground floor).

A meeting was arranged with the head and a professional advisor or 'friend' in July 1994. A regional representative of Martin's professional association visited him several times together with his local representative in school. They eventually persuaded him that his only alternative was to take retirement on the grounds of ill health. He agreed. The head and head of department continued to monitor his performance, but his retirement was agreed for December 1994.

This outcome would be less likely to happen now. Retirement was agreed on the grounds of chronic pain in his leg. The fact that he had been able to return to school and was able to walk seemed to show that this was no longer a serious enough problem to merit early retirement. It is likely that continual absence would have eventually have led to dismissal because of unfitness to teach. It is also likely now that action would have been taken at an earlier stage, probably starting with Martin's induction into teaching, and the effect of the subsequent role change would be closely monitored as part of the support given in the early stages of the capability procedures.

Sometimes a member of staff's effectiveness is reduced while medication is being regulated to suit their particular needs. A normally effective senior teacher was finding it difficult to cope with the demands of her job. She felt exhausted and tearful and was forcing herself to go into school each day. Anything unexpected caused her to panic for fear of not having the energy to deal effectively with the extra demands made on her. She eventually consulted her doctor and found that the cause was in fact medical, a thyroid malfunction. Her effectiveness remained reduced while the best course of treatment was worked out and settled into, but both she and her managers were prepared to accept the poorer performance in the short term, confident that she would resume her role effectively as soon as possible. Their confidence was well-founded, as she was functioning again as normal by the end of the term.

It is not always possible for a member of staff to continue in the same role once a chronic, debilitating medical condition has been diagnosed. An excellent head of modern languages began to suffer from lack of feeling in her arms and was diagnosed as having multiple sclerosis. She spent a short time in hospital for tests to ascertain the correct medication, diet and exercise routine for her needs, then returned to school. For a while she was able to maintain her level of effectiveness but, after about eighteen months, had to admit, very unwillingly, that her job was too demanding. She agreed to relinquish her head of department responsibilities, thus enabling a colleague to develop into the role, and for several years was able to continue working full-time as a teacher. At one point in this time it became necessary for her to move to a teaching room on the ground floor and she changed her teaching style to more directly whole-class activities so that she could continue working without moving around more than absolutely necessary. Eventually, to everyone's great sadness, she was unable to walk well enough to continue to function in school and was granted early retirement. In her case the only real period of poor performance was while her illness was being diagnosed and medication tested. For the rest of the time the whole school, staff and pupils together, worked with her to achieve the best for everyone. This was a learning situation that had far wider value than just effective teaching of modern languages.

New staff

Newly appointed staff at all levels and in all areas are particularly likely to experience a period of poor performance. When a vacancy occurs in industry or commerce, the cost of the time necessary for the replacement to learn the skills of the job is included in the costs of recruitment. It is acknowledged that there has to be a learning period during which production or sales may not reach the normal level. In education, there is some acceptance of this where newly qualified teachers are concerned, but little or none where the new member of staff is already experienced, even if, as is most likely, their experience is in a different post in a different school or college. They are usually highly motivated to succeed and will do whatever they can to ensure success but sometimes circumstances are beyond their control.

Traditional selection and recruitment methods are notoriously inaccurate as indicators of success in the relevant post as, in general, they do not target the skills and attributes that are actually needed in the job. Today there is a greater tendency to integrate some active demonstration of teaching skills into the process of selecting a teacher but the process still does not test time management, organisational skills and good people management skills. The impression candidates give at interview may, however unintentionally, be different from the reality of their professional performance. This does not indicate that their performance is automatically worse than expected, but that the strengths that are displayed by successful candidates at interview can be different from those required in the classroom or in management. A delightfully articulate extrovert may impress the selection committee but fail to plan and deliver a coherent module of work. Similarly, in a management role this candidate may lack the skills necessary to manage change.

Much of the responsibility for poor performance in newly appointed staff rests with the appointing school or college: once a member of staff has been appointed. How effective is their induction programme? How well is the new member of staff briefed about the culture of the establishment (or, indeed, the change in culture which the head and governors may be looking to initiate through new appointments)? Are the expectations of both sides transparent? Sometimes problems can easily be solved by better and more complete communication. One head of department felt at a loss because he had not been given the calendar of meetings for the school year, and it was not until he had missed a first curriculum committee meeting that he was aware that he lacked the information. He would also have liked to have been briefed on the likely cycle of topics of these meetings so that he could discuss issues in his department first. Established staff had learned when decisions were likely to be made about perennial topics such as the Key Stage 4 curriculum or arrangements for open days, but these were new to him and he felt unable to perform as well as he wished as a manager because he lacked some basic information about the rhythms within the school.

Newly qualified teaching staff

Sometimes the head and governors are forced into making an appointment about which they have reservations. In some areas and in some subjects it is very difficult to recruit staff of the hoped for quality. (This is also true of administrative staff and is dealt with in more depth below.) It has never been easy to recruit modern linguists, and the situation has been exacerbated since the introduction of the National Curriculum. It is even worse if a dual linguist is required, and worse still if this is mid-year.

Wayne

Wayne's predecessor in post was due to start her maternity leave in November. She taught French and German throughout the school. An advertisement for someone to cover her maternity leave had been published early in the term and had brought no response at all. So the department worked together to reallocate examination classes wherever possible and set work for those that had to be covered by a supply teacher.

Not wanting to risk being short of a specialist linguist for an indefinite period, and knowing that the number of language classes would be greater in September, the head persuaded her governors to take the risk of advertising for a linguist on a two-term contract in the first instance, but with the possibility of a permanent contract for a suitable candidate. This new advertisement brought in three applications. Interviews took place. One candidate failed to turn up. Of the other two, only one had qualifications in both French and German but was not a qualified teacher. Wayne had been working as an English teacher in France and in Germany since leaving university in Germany. His qualifications afforded him graduate status but not qualified teacher status. The head had therefore to assess the extra cost of taking a member of staff through this route. The LEA would carry the cost of necessary training, but the school would have to allocate time to a mentor as well as substantial non-contact time to Wayne for lesson observation and training. There was the additional complication that, having agreed to appoint Wayne, the school had a duty to give him a year's contract while obtaining qualified status. The head concluded that there was really no other option available and Wayne had the extra advantage of being able to start work almost immediately.

The head allocated a senior member of staff to the role of mentor, who would work closely with an adviser to plan a programme for Wayne. At first it seemed that the decision had been a good one. Wayne's honeymoon period lasted to the end of term; classes were thankful to have a teacher who was a subject specialist after a diet of worksheets supervised by supply teachers. Not long after the beginning of the spring term, the head of department found herself dealing with problems of discipline in Wayne's classes. Closer examination of the causes showed up problems with lesson planning and classroom management with which Wayne did not seem to be coming to grips. His mentor spent a lot of time working with him on basic strategies. The INSET he attended externally also focused on the basics but he did not seem to be making any progress.

By Easter the head had to make a decision about Wayne's future in the school, either to keep him on through the next year (to avoid a repetition of the current scenario) or to allow his contract to expire while recruiting someone to replace him in September. The original teacher decided not to return after her maternity leave. The head's decision was a difficult one to make as it involved making assumptions about Wayne's likely progress in the next term. So she solicited LEA advice. They advised her to retain Wayne, their view being that there was a continuing shortage of language teachers and that he was likely to improve sufficiently to become a satisfactory teacher. The head of department was not of the same opinion – she was tiring of spending so much time supporting Wayne to the disadvantage of other pupils' language learning. The head decided that the head of department had the stronger claim, so advertised for a new linguist for the autumn term.

Although this had the immediate effect of demoralising Wayne, it also made him realise that he needed to assess his own situation and his real potential as a teacher. The LEA advisor was still able to support him and would help him work towards obtaining another post, with the result that he made serious efforts to succeed. When the time came for interviews to be held for the new post Wayne had sufficiently improved to be included among the candidates and turned out to be the successful one.

This scenario shows that the clear message given by the head made a potentially failing teacher turn the situation around. The strength of the head was also shown in her willingness to acknowledge that the situation had changed and to appoint Wayne to the substantive post.

Sometimes the newly qualified teacher is obviously not going to succeed as a teacher. The period since the probationary year was abolished has been a particularly difficult one, without the flexibility afforded by probation. This has been partially overcome by more newly qualified teachers being appointed on temporary contracts in the first instance, but this is not always an option where there is a shortage of candidates for a post. When she observed a lesson he delivered, one headteacher was very relieved that the decision had been to appoint a Latin teacher on a two-term contract in the first instance. The teacher had been so preoccupied on entering the room that he did not notice that the curtains were closed and he conducted the whole lesson in the darkness behind an overhead projector. He did not realise that the pupils, to whom he did not directly speak during the whole lesson, could not see him and the blackboard. This person was an able classicist but had no idea how to transfer his knowledge to the pupils. A great deal of support over the two terms in which he worked at the school did not succeed in enabling him to overcome this problem. His contract was not renewed and he was advised to think carefully about whether he had chosen the right career.

Languages are not the only area in which there can be difficulties of recruitment. Often problems are experienced in recruiting good quality teachers of maths, science and technology. Since the beginning of the current recession, a lot of engineers and computer specialists have taken the opportunity to train as teachers. Many have found the career change to be the best decision they have ever made, thoroughly stimulated by the new environment and the satisfaction of seeing pupils learn, and bringing a new dimension to the school or college in which they are working. Others have found the transition more difficult, as the case studies of Marcus (Chapter 9) and Lorraine show.

Lorraine

Lorraine's post in a scientific research company had been made redundant. After some time failing to obtain another similar post, she decided to take a PGCE and apply for a teaching post. The reference provided by the college was a bland statement of the course elements and an acknowledgement that Lorraine had satisfactorily completed the course. She was duly appointed to a post in a mixed comprehensive along with several other newly qualified teachers. This school provided a good induction course and mentors for new staff so Lorraine was well supported, and also closely monitored from the beginning. It soon became clear to her colleagues that Lorraine did not relate well to pupils and seemed unable to deliver lessons pitched at the right level. This inevitably resulted in disruptive behaviour. At all stages Lorraine was given feedback about her work and constructive suggestions for improvement, but she did not really improve. She was very unwilling to admit that she was not performing satisfactorily, perhaps afraid of losing her job for a second time, and tried to hide the problems. By Christmas she had made no real progress and, as there was substantial evidence of poor performance, the headteacher decided to begin informal capability procedures. Finally understanding that the situation was serious, Lorraine resigned. If she had not done so it is likely that she would have been dismissed by the end of the year.

In such cases it does not seem good for either the school or the individual for procedures to be protracted. Clear support had been given from the beginning and no progress was made. It was better that Lorraine accepted that secondary school teaching was not for her as soon as possible, so that she could rethink her career and move on.

Experienced staff moving to different schools

School culture and expectations are often the reasons for poor performance when staff move to different schools. Often there seems to be an assumption that the new member of staff will automatically slip into the totality of the role vacated. In the case study of Jane (Chapter 9), although she was not newly appointed to the school, in a way she was like a new member of staff finding herself in this kind of situation. Neither she, nor the staff year team she took over, realised that there would need to be a period of adjustment while necessary changes were acknowledged and made.

Sometimes the previous incumbent vacates the post physically but leaves a potentially overwhelming burden for the new member of staff (see the example of Steve in Chapter 9). This could be a burden of expectations, as for Jane, but it could be a budget deficit or a commitment to expenditure on resources that the new leader would not have chosen. It could also be the pressure of pupils' expectations: that certain clubs happen on certain days after school; that homework is presented in a particular way; or that negative behaviour is dealt with in a specific way that seems idiosyncratic to the new leader. All these limit the freedom of the new leader to develop his or her own style and lead the team effectively.

It is not only the mismatch between interview skills and the skills of a successful teacher and manager that can lead to poor performance, but also a lack of appreciation that the skills exercised successfully in a previous role are not necessarily the ones that will be needed in the new role. The case of Steve illustrates both this point and that made in the paragraph above.

It is particularly difficult for newly recruited heads of department to be sure of success in the new environment. Most schools have induction programmes for newly qualified teachers and new recruits into senior management usually find support within the management team, but heads of department are often left to settle in on their own after the initial meetings for new staff. They have no obvious close colleagues until they have established a rapport with the people working in their departments so, until they have understood the dynamics pertaining to the heads of department group, do they work in collaboration or in competition with each other?

The two very different scenarios below illustrate the debilitating effect of a change of culture and the weight of either one's own or other people's expectations of experienced teachers moving into a management role in a different school. For a new manager, there is no opportunity to stand back and look at the specific role from outside before having to take it on completely. In most other jobs or professions there would be a period of acclimatisation to allow new colleagues to see how things are done and learn the procedures before actively taking on the new role. But in teaching, the whole job is taken on from day one, any mistakes are made in full view of colleagues (and pupils) and it can be difficult to re-establish the desired position once mistakes have been made. It is unfortunately true that a first impression can only be made once.

Alice

Alice had come into education from industry. She was well-qualified and was recruited to a maths post in the mixed grammar school where she had been a pupil. She thoroughly enjoyed her first year in teaching, started a chess club and was promoted as soon as an opportunity arose. She was particularly interested in the most able pupils, developing their interest in more advanced areas of mathematics and regularly working with small groups after school. She was therefore very enthusiastic about promotion to a post she saw advertised in a comprehensive school that was looking for a mathematician with a special interest in developing work with more able pupils. She put in a good application and was appointed. She was not, however, prepared for the change in culture and working practices in her new environment and decided to resign at the end of the first term. She had never experienced life in a comprehensive school; after being a grammar school pupil she had gone to university and then into industry, then to a grammar school for her teaching practice prior to obtaining the post back in her old school. To her the contrasts were stark:

In the grammar school:	In the comprehensive school:
Pupils seated to face the teacher	Pupils seated in groups
Older, established teaching team	Young teaching team
Experienced managers at all levels	Inexperienced managers except the head
Large amount of sixth form teaching	Little sixth form teaching
Few meetings	Huge number of meetings
Time to run clubs after school	Meetings after school

Alice decided that she would stay in education but would immediately seek a post back in a selective or independent school. She was supported in this decision by the head of the comprehensive school, who was impressed by Alice's integrity. Alice did not want to allow the mismatch of her expectations, and the reality as she saw it to affect her work with pupils, so she resigned before her performance deteriorated. She was fortunate to be able to resign; most people would probably have had no option but to remain trapped in the situation. When headteachers are weighing up the implications of supporting a teacher like Alice in the search for another post, it is important to acknowledge that success or failure in one environment does not necessarily imply a similar outcome in a different one.

Rob

Rob's fresh approach and genuine enthusiasm impressed the interviewing panel. He was the only man being interviewed and was at least ten years younger than the others. The English department for which he would be taking responsibility was made up of women at least ten years older than himself. The only anxiety the interviewing panel had was whether to take the safe option and appoint someone in the same mould as the rest of the department, or to go for change by appointing Rob. They appointed Rob.

The rest of the department was delighted that this pleasant young man would be joining them. They were all hard-working, successful teachers whose confidence had been rather undermined by the huge changes in the English curriculum and the impossibility of devising satisfactory ways of teaching and assessing it before being overtaken by another set of changes. Under the previous head of department their pupils achieved excellent examination results, but she had become disillusioned as the implications of the National Curriculum unfolded. She had eventually decided to leave teaching altogether rather than try to implement a curriculum with which she fundamentally disagreed. This left the department feeling very anxious and in need of someone who had really got to grips with the new requirements.

Rob's problem turned out not to be the new requirements but the tutor group and department he took over from the previous head of department. Year 11 pupils are not easy to win over and a young man in a previously all-women area was easy prey for them. The members of the department were looking for leadership from him, but were witnessing problems with class control and discipline. They were looking for the impossible: they wanted a strong man as leader but tended to treat Rob like their young son. For Rob, the situation was a complete disaster and he began to consider resigning.

From a senior management point of view, Rob's performance in his new role was poor and it seemed as though they had made a bad decision in appointing him. There were problems of discipline in the department requiring intervention by one deputy head and problems with meeting deadlines for assessments and documentation that concerned the other deputy. This deputy was Rob's mentor. At first Rob was reluctant to talk to her about his problems, but gradually he realised that she knew exactly what the situation was and wanted to help him succeed. They started off by listing exactly what the problems were, deciding which ones needed immediate attention and which could be worked on more slowly. They decided that his credibility in the department was dependent on his successful relationship with the tutor group. The focal point of his difficulties with the group was a girl who had caused problems with several members of staff, but who had felt strongly supported by the previous head of department and who felt very let down by her departure. Individual pupil counselling during year 11 was a feature of the school, so the deputy agreed with Rob to work with this particular pupil as if it was part of the normal counselling scheme, thus giving her support while Rob worked with the rest of the group. This was only a small change but it helped the dynamics of the group become less hostile and enabled Rob to begin to establish himself sufficiently to be adequately effective, if not popular, with the group for the short time they had left in the school.

Required documentation was then prioritised and to some extent simplified, leaving more time for discussion with the rest of the department about how they wanted work to be assessed. This release from some deadlines also helped Rob develop ways of working with his department staff to share understanding of new issues. It was a slow process, but by the end of the year Rob's confidence was returning and he began to lead his department effectively. He also had the opportunity later that year to be involved in the appointment of two new teachers, a man and a woman, who only knew him as the head of department.

Rob's difficult position was somewhat relieved by a changing staffing situation and by the departure of his tutor group, but his development would still need support and monitoring. How effective would he be with a new tutor group? Would he succeed in making up lost time on his departmental documentation? More importantly, how did the teachers in the department respond to his ways of involving them in developing assessment in English? And, therefore, how successful was he becoming as a head of department? The potential for poor performance is not usually removed overnight, but schools in which there is a positive ethos for staff development supported by a sound framework for monitoring performance are in a good position to minimise or even prevent it altogether.

Established staff

Demands of the job have changed but the member of staff has not kept up with these changes

Career life-cycle research identifies a critical mid-career period when people who have been in post for a while assess their situation and either find a new way of motivating themselves or begin to stagnate. The decision to do either of these is usually in response to personal, internal factors but is often triggered by an imminent or enforced change in their professional situation. This is a recurring theme across schools where new headteachers have recently taken over. They find (and/or a recent OFSTED inspection finds) that their least effective members of staff are in their forties and fifties and have been in the school a long time. They generally define 'least effective' in terms of test and examination results that are consistently below average for the school, and in terms of paperwork and planning that has not been updated to comply with the current expectations for their subject or key stage. These are the issues on which schools are measured and compared and from which improvement targets are set.

Quantifiable criteria and a focus on outcomes are comparatively new to education, and these teachers have not been used to thinking of their work in these terms. They established their own criteria at a time when teachers were appointed and then left to get on with the job with considerable autonomy. They probably ran clubs after school and the occasional trip out for their pupils and felt, quite rightly, that they were doing their best for the children in their care. They did not notice that, as the years went by, they introduced new topics less frequently, or they took less pride in keeping their marking up to date, having marked the same material many times over their years in post. They had noticed that a lot of changes were happening in education but were not prepared to leap onto bandwagons, preferring to wait and see before making changes themselves. This was probably reinforced by at least some members of senior management, who fitted into the same category themselves. It is only when a new head is appointed that new criteria for effectiveness are applied and the shortcomings of such teachers are identified. The challenge for the new head is in dealing with the justifiable response of such teachers that no one had ever suggested before that their work was unacceptable.

Sometimes a member of staff will refuse to make the changes seen as necessary by the new leader:

Olwen

For as long as anyone else on the staff could remember, Olwen had taught the year 6 class in the big classroom next to the staffroom. No one had considered it worth arguing about, although other teachers would have liked the opportunity to teach that year group. A new headteacher and an OFSTED inspection were both about to happen to the school, and the new head had been advised by the LEA that OFSTED would find a lot to criticise in the school. The long-established staff had taken little notice of the National Curriculum, believing that it was a 'fad' that would fade away, and this opinion had been reinforced by the constant refocusing of its requirements. It was a small school, and they had got on with their individual work over the years with little interruption from outside.

The new head had been appointed by the governors with a mandate to make radical changes. There was no time to work slowly with the staff. Pupils were not receiving their entitlement, and the head had been warned that Olwen would be the most difficult to persuade to make changes. After interviews with staff and an assessment of the situation, he decided that a symbolic indication of change was needed. Thus, he announced that teachers were invited to submit requests for teaching groups and rooms for the following year. Olwen announced that she would be having year 6 in room 1 as usual. The head replied that that would not be possible, Olwen's request would be considered along with everyone else's, but he was intending to allocate rooms in a way that better suited a variety of teaching and learning strategies. Olwen had been used to having her own way, so she indicated that she would resign if she was not allocated her class and her room. The head did not allocate them to her. She resigned as the preparations for the new year were being finalised.

To a large extent, Olwen's resignation opened up other opportunities for change and avoided unnecessary confrontation. Olwen had three options for action: to resign, to remain adamant that she would not accept the changes, or to accept the head's proposal. The head knew that all three possible outcomes would enable him to enact his mandate. He had made it clear that changes were going to be implemented. He had the right to insist on reasonable changes; these were reasonable changes and Olwen had no right to refuse to comply. If she had continued to refuse rather than resign, the head and governors would have had the right to start disciplinary procedures against her. It is not clear whether Olwen's performance as a teacher was actually below standard, but it is likely from our knowledge of the school that the National Curriculum was not being properly taught, that deficiencies were present and that the extent of these deficiencies would be confirmed by the OFSTED inspection. It is likely that Olwen took the opportunity to resign on a matter of principle before having to face criticism of her work, and that she felt unable to deal with the likely imposed changes after not making any changes for so many years. Her resignation opened up opportunities for other staff as well as making it clear to them that the head had firm expectations of them all. (The third possible outcome was for Olwen to accept the teaching group and room he proposed for her and thus concur with his decision.)

After the OFSTED inspection, other members of staff expressed support for the changes that had prevented the possibility of serious repercussions (special measures) and there was considerable appreciation of the courage the headteacher had shown in dealing firmly with the problem.

This kind of situation can exist at any level of management as well as with the classroom teacher. The case of Graham (Chapter 9) is one that highlights the complexities inherent in dealing with someone whose performance is perceived to be poor across several functions. Some of the problems are caused by Graham's failure to keep up with changes. The reasons for the problems continuing are partly because he is unable to grasp some of the new concepts, but also because he has fallen so far behind that the effort required to catch up is likely to be beyond him.

Sometimes there is a solution to the problem that reinvents the member of staff in a completely new role

Most of the following cases could be looked at equally in the section focusing on staff in management positions, as it is from these positions that it is easier to find ways of remotivating a poorly performing member of staff. Max (Chapter 9) was given the opportunity to lead new work on the financial side of school management, and Wynn (Chapter 9) was able to change the priorities of his role to enable him to continue to work successfully. The same was true in the case of Erica.

Erica

Erica had been head of geography in the local high school since 1980. As a young teacher she had been totally immersed in her work, believing her subject to be utterly fascinating and seeing no reason to go outside it for stimulation. She lived alone. Her weekends and holidays were often spent taking pupils on local rambling expeditions and on holidays in youth hostels in Britain and abroad. She was heavily involved in the Duke of Edinburgh awards. She went everywhere by bicycle or train and had neither time, nor interest, to learn to drive a car. When she became head of department after ten years in teaching, she moved from the next-door school and was already well-known in the town for her enthusiastic approach to geography teaching.

Over the next ten years or so, very little changed. Erica continued to be motivated by the proactive side of her work. As a head of department she made changes such as an update in the textbooks used in the department, and agreed the distribution of classes with the other two geography teachers (it was quite simple as the school regularly had six forms of entry and everyone studied geography). At first that really was almost all that was needed and Erica, though an enthusiastic practitioner, was not the type of person to have new ideas or seek change.

By the early 1990s, however, a lot was changing around her. She made some adjustments in the direction of the National Curriculum and generally continued with what she enjoyed doing best. She was very popular with both pupils and parents, whom she reminded of the favourite teachers from their own schooldays, so was genuinely unaware that her work was gradually becoming both out of date and was being carried out to a slowly deteriorating standard.

As so often happens, it was the combination of a new headteacher and an impending inspection that raised management awareness of Erica's performance. The LEA pre-OFSTED 'health check' revealed that she was falling far short of expected standards both as a classroom teacher and as a head of department. In the classroom she was using a limited range of teaching techniques, used out-of-date materials, had been setting unchallenging and often inappropriate homework and had done very little marking. That which she had done was perfunctory and undevelopmental. As a head of department she was responsible for the materials used by the department and for developing schemes of work appropriate to the new requirements: this had not been done. The LEA inspectors praised the school's highly successful programme of field trips and their Duke of Edinburgh scheme which attracted higher numbers of participants than any other maintained school in the authority. This was almost exclusively Erica's work.

There were obviously many ways in which Erica was an asset, particularly in areas that helped give the school its particular character and which were highly valued by parents. Losing these could potentially be more obviously and immediately damaging to the school than a poor inspection report on the standards of teaching and learning in the geography department, but the fact that pupils were entitled to a better quality learning experience could not be ignored.

Erica was shocked by the feedback she received. Geography was her life. At first she strongly denied that she was failing in any way, asserting, quite truthfully, that no one had found fault with her work before. But the evidence was there and she eventually accepted that she had, perhaps subconsciously, allowed her standards to slip in those areas that no longer motivated her or that she had not realised were essential while she deployed her time and energy in the areas she enjoyed. She did not want to be seen as a failure and was more than willing to find ways forward.

Unfortunately, little more than a damage limitation exercise could be carried out before the OFSTED inspection and the report did indeed criticise the standards in the geography department, but a longer-term solution was required. It was really too late for Erica to learn and implement the wide-ranging changes in the geography curriculum while also updating her own teaching skills. Happily, another solution was possible in this particular case. The teacher responsible for examination administration was moving away from the area. She was a history teacher. One of the other geography teachers was also moving to another post. This created the possibility of Erica taking on responsibility for examinations if the third teacher in the department was willing to teach some history, leaving an opportunity for the appointment of a new head of geography.

This arrangement suited everybody. Erica would learn a new role while updating her teaching skills and continuing to organise the trips and Award scheme that actually provided her with personal satisfaction and her status in the school and its community. No one lost face and developmental opportunities became available for others as well.

On the surface this seems too good to be true, as the right opportunities do not often appear when needed, but it is a good example of the possibilities that can arise from lateral thinking by good management. When a vacancy occurs on a school staff, it is always a good moment to take an overview of the whole school. After reflection and discussion there might actually be no alternative but to fill, in its totality, the actual vacancy that was created. It might be, on the other hand, the opportunity to make changes not directly connected with the vacancy but able to be enacted thanks to it being there as a catalyst. If, as in this case, the teacher does have skills that are important to the school in its wider educational role, there is no point in losing such skills if there is a way in which they can be retained.

One senior teacher moved from being head of sixth form to responsibility for assessment and another to work with new intake and induction. The latter had been head of sixth form for fifteen years and was very anxious about the risks he ran in changing his role, especially in terms of status, but he found in working with younger pupils and their parents and the feeder schools a source of renewed enthusiasm. In primary schools it is less easy to find ways of revitalising someone's role: fewer opportunities crop up in terms of vacancies, and the largest part of the role will remain in the classroom whatever other changes are made.

Support and administrative staff are also prone to reaching a stage in their careers where they have probably lost touch with changing demands or have lost interest in developing because the workload has increased beyond their ability to cope. These issues will be dealt with in a later section.

For the classroom teacher, the problem is less easy to resolve. In primary schools, a change in year group can be revitalising, as can a change in subject responsibility. These changes require prioritising staff development funds. This may be a difficult decision to make where budgets are small and other members of staff already have the skills required. It raises the issue of under-performing staff apparently being rewarded for poor work, and needs to be part of an overall development plan in which all staff are seen to have opportunities for development.

Sometimes the member of staff has actually been performing at a low level for a long time

In this situation the member of staff may not be competent to make the necessary improvements, and the only solution then is removal from the post, and probably the profession. This removal could be through early retirement, retirement through ill health, or dismissal because of lack of capability. It is not always possible to take remedial action or to find another role in which the person would be sure to function satisfactorily. Sometimes colleagues have become weary of carrying the responsibility of someone who is not carrying out their share of the workload to the standard required, so, in spite of the natural, humane feelings towards the relevant person, they are relieved of a great deal of pressure when the underperforming colleague goes.

Physics teacher

The physics teacher had come into education from industry when he was approaching forty and his career was not progressing. That was almost twenty years ago, at a point when physics teachers were particularly difficult to recruit. From the beginning there had been problems, according to the file of parents' complaints in the head's office. Parents had complained of bad behaviour in the classroom, that pupils were sometimes left alone in the lab, that results were poor so few pupils opted for physics at GCSE or 'A' level. The head of science at the time did not see his role as monitoring work of colleagues so nothing had been done to improve the situation until a new head and new head of science took up posts. Immediately job descriptions were discussed and clarified so everyone in the department knew what was expected of them. Everyone was given some aspect of the department's work to monitor and short-term targets were set.

The physics teacher ignored these. It seemed he was hoping that no one would insist on change as he was only two years from retirement age. But the head did insist and arranged a meeting with the teacher to look at the targets he had been set and to make it clear that he was expected to meet these. Support and training were put in place and the teacher was informed that capability procedures would be set in motion if the targets were not met.

During the next term the deputy head regularly observed lessons (at first by prior arrangement then without warning) and at a meeting with the head it was agreed that there was a noticeable improvement and some targets were being met (being in the classroom on time, making a proper start and end to each lesson, marking done properly according to the policies and practices of the department). Because of this improvement it was decided not to continue with capability procedures.

The next term an LEA science adviser was invited to assess the situation. He found it to be as bad as it had been a term earlier: still little marking being done, still parents complaining about poor teaching. Once the pressure had been taken off, the teacher had discontinued the improved practice. So the informal process had to be repeated, as briefly as possible but still taking time before formal procedures could be started. The teacher contacted his professional association, who advised him to resign. By the end of the term he would be only six months short of sixty so they suggested he would lose very little by resigning and could risk losing a lot if he ended up being dismissed.

Under the new capability expectations the head could move much more quickly with this teacher, with such a body of evidence against him, even after the delay caused by the slight improvement. However, there is always going to be a grey area around those members of staff who can improve their performance to an acceptable level in some areas. Do you extend targets when all but one of them are met? How much time and effort from all parties concerned is to be expended on keeping performance at a level that is no more than acceptable? How can targets reached this year be extended as the standard of performance in the whole school improves?

One primary school teacher had been the subject of the informal stage of capability procedures twice, under two different headteachers. Each time there seemed to have been adequate improvement so procedures were discontinued but the quality of performance gradually deteriorated again and re-establishing the informal procedures was delayed because of a change of headteacher. The second time, prior to an OFSTED inspection, a great deal of effort was put in by senior staff, particularly the English co-ordinator, to coach the teacher through the inspection. Afterwards the English co-ordinator was no longer able to make this teacher a priority and there was yet another change of head. At first it looked as though the problem would be resolved by a family move abroad but this did not happen and the new head felt she could no longer overlook the teacher's poor attitude towards pupils, which was belittling, with ceaselessly negative comments. Even the caretaker was heard to mention that the teacher disliked children. This time, formal procedures were set in motion with a firm intention to dismiss unless substantial and sustained improvements were made.

Sometimes lack of awareness of the magnitude of change can affect the work of a complete department:

History department

The history department of a small grammar school consisted of two teachers whose combined length of service in the school totalled forty-eight years. The 'A' level results had never been outstanding and had not improved in line with improvements across the rest of the school. It was also the only department not to be increasing in line with the increase in the number of pupils, especially in the sixth form, as fewer pupils opted for history at GCSE level and even fewer at 'A' level.

A new head was appointed with a brief to improve standards in the school but also to effect staff reductions to overcome serious financial problems. The head of history was identified for redundancy as he was the only member of staff unwilling or unable to teach a second subject. History was then made the responsibility of an overall head of humanities faculty who was asked to work with the other history teacher to improve standards in history. It was discovered that this teacher was still using some of the same teaching notes she had prepared on taking up post over twenty years previously. Neither she nor the head of department had attended INSET to keep up to date with changes in the history curriculum and were barely aware of changes to the syllabuses they taught. The head of faculty agreed targets with the history teacher to be met within the next school year. These were all based on up-to-date planning and delivery of the subject to ensure the best possible outcomes for the current cohorts of pupils, with a view to looking at methodology the following year. Classroom control and discipline were not problems in this school.

In this case the teacher did not achieve the targets set and the head, with evidence from the head of faculty, set formal capability procedures in motion. As soon as these began the teacher resigned, but not without there being substantial concerns expressed by other members of staff. There was some feeling that too much pressure was being exerted by the head to the detriment of individual members of staff and staff morale in general. The history department had not been the only area in which, for whatever reason, necessary changes had been ignored or overlooked, and the perceived summary removal of both teachers in one subject area caused ripples of anxiety across the school. In the short term the effect was divisive and unsettling, but it had the medium-term effect of causing the large number of teachers in the mid-career transition zone to find new motivation or to leave. In the longer term the head's strategy led to a noticeable improvement in examination grades across all areas and a widening of teaching and learning experiences for the pupils. Reaching this successful outcome was painful for everyone involved.

Middle management positions (including deputy headteachers)

Staff in management positions may exhibit symptoms of poor performance under most of the circumstances described and explored in the first three parts of this section: temporary poor performance caused by a change in team membership (Jane), problems caused by medical conditions (head of Modern Languages suffering from multiple sclerosis), and difficulties in adapting to circumstances in new schools (Steve, Alice and Rob). They may also, as in the case of Erica, be long-established staff who have not kept up with the changes required of them in their roles. Most of the full case studies in Chapter 9 have been chosen because of the complex or multiple issues surrounding perceived poor performance. It therefore follows that most of them also focus on staff in management positions.

As was seen when looking at possible problems with new staff coming into a school in positions of responsibility, there are many reasons why they may perform below the expected standard. Success as a classroom teacher does not guarantee success in a management role. The requirements of the two are quite different; hence the ongoing debate about rewarding excellent classroom practitioners financially rather than promoting them out of the classroom. As can be seen in the cases of Alice and Rob above, success in a particular role in one school does not ensure success in a different school. A well-planned selection process followed up with a comprehensive induction programme should be effective in avoiding too many of these cases happening, but sometimes difficulties in recruiting staff with the skills needed for a particular job can lead to problems after the appointment:

Neville

At a time when business studies teachers were in short supply, the head was persuaded to appoint Neville from a post in further education to head of business studies because he also had IT skills. Unfortunately, he lacked the ability to impart knowledge. A senior teacher was the other business studies teacher. She felt that his lessons were woolly with no focus and no clear objectives, and parents soon began to complain to her that their sixth form sons and daughters found they could not understand business concepts and did not seem to be covering the syllabus. Furthermore, marking seemed to be irregular and very sketchily completed.

In the meantime, Neville seemed to create an aura of difficulty in IT, discouraging other staff from involving themselves in an area that seemed too difficult to be worth the effort required to gain access to and making his own skills seem indispensable. For a while the head felt she needed to accept the underperformance in business studies for fear of losing the precious IT possibilities. She had none of these skills herself, so could not gauge the risk she would run by losing this teacher.

A temporary solution offered itself in the form of reorganisation of the school administration with the advent of local management and information systems for school administration. The head offered Neville a brief secondment into the school office to set up the systems, retaining a small teaching commitment in IT only.

When the secondment was over Neville moved back into business studies but teaching a GNVQ instead of 'A' level. Working within the tight guidelines of the GNVQ the problem seemed to have been solved, but it was only hidden. It turned out that a few pupils returning for examination certificates discovered that some they had expected to find were not included in their envelopes. Neville responded that they had not been provided by the examining board. Further enquiry revealed that the board had not received evidence for the award of the qualification. Work was discovered, unmarked, in Neville's office. He quickly marked it but the board returned it as having not been properly marked.

The head responded to this with an oral warning resulting from dereliction of duty. Neville's professional association felt he had been very lightly dealt with and, knowing the weight of other complaints received, persuaded him that early retirement (he was in his early fifties) would avoid any likely repercussions.

This response is no longer an obvious option as it is dependent on LEAs and/or governors to carry the cost of early retirement, and in this case there had been so many problems that the governors would probably not view such expenditure sympathetically. Now, such a case could probably qualify for the 'fast track' capability procedure, or for misconduct, as so much evidence had already built up towards dismissal.

Success as a curriculum or pastoral team leader does not necessarily transfer to success in a senior management role where a wider view is required.

The small rural primary school was shocked by the findings of its OFSTED inspection team, who identified low achievement and poor management as key issues for development. These were particularly in respect of SEN provision and teaching at Key Stage 1. The deputy head was both SENCO and Key Stage 1 co-ordinator. He was also identified as a weak teacher and had relationship difficulties with colleagues.

Monitoring visits from the LEA over the next year found no evidence of real improvement in spite of support and training opportunities, but the head was held back by a substantial segment of the governing body who were very anxious about the effect on the school of embarking on the capability procedures. The LEA strongly supported the head and the governors were eventually persuaded.

Eighteen months after the inspection, formal procedures began. The informal stages were deemed to have been already completed in light of the urgency of the situation. Very clear targets were set, such as:

- hand in planning on time every week
- ensure all pupils are on the SEN register by a set date
- organise the classroom so that there is clear labelling of areas
- complete reading progress sheets as agreed school practice

These targets had to be met within six weeks. Absence through illness caused delay in this, but the extended targets were still not met. They were renewed and monitored by the LEA through classroom observation. At the next review six weeks later they still had not been met so, although the deputy head was now permanently on sick leave, a formal governors' committee was set up. They received evidence of lack of capability, heard his professional representative's concerns about his state of health and decided to dismiss him. He did not appeal against this.

In this case it feels as though there had been a knee-jerk reaction to the OFSTED report, laying the blame for a poor report on one member of staff who happened to hold key roles in the school. But it is also likely that in such a small school, one particularly ineffective teacher/manager would have a disproportionate influence on standards achieved. There was, however, substantial evidence of continuing poor performance during the period after the inspection, thus justifying the formal action, but also paving the way for more widespread evaluation of the work of the school. The report had come as a surprise to everyone. What was the role of the head in this? Had this made her evaluate her own skills as a manager? What about the other classroom teachers? Would they be able to face up to the changes they would be required to make? Would there in fact be others involved in formal procedures before the school began to make real improvements? And what effect was all this having on the pupils, both present and future, and their parents, and thus the reputation of the school?

The performance of a deputy head can directly influence the perceived performance of a headteacher, since the deputy's role is often to work with the rest of the staff to implement the head's management decisions. If the deputy is not competent to do this, or, even worse, unwilling to do this, then the head is not likely to succeed in leading the school forward. We have been told of many cases where a new head has found working with an established deputy head to be the most difficult part of his or her new role. This does not necessarily mean that such deputies are poor performers, but adapting to working under new leadership challenges both their willingness and their ability to change. Often, dealing with what turns out to be poor performance is also difficult for the head who must acquire objective evidence and avoid accusations of allowing differences in personality and style to influence judgements about performance.

This is further complicated by the fact that one must assume that, to have reached deputy headship, performance must have been at least satisfactory for most of the person's career and that the person is probably also well-known and respected in the local community. The role of deputy head requires a broader spectrum of skills than may have been necessary for appointments made before the changes of the last decade. Unwilling to risk visible failure, some deputies retreat behind the mask of the timetable or new information systems, claiming their responsibility for one of these is all they have time for. All these issues are explored under other headings, but are brought into sharper focus when the perceived poor performer plays such a high profile role and has responsibility for the work of so many other people.

As in the case of the failing department, poor performance by a classroom teacher may in fact be the result of a poorly performing manager at whatever level within the system. It is therefore extremely important that the causes of poor performance are explored thoroughly so that preventive or remedial action can be accurately targeted.

Teaching support staff

Introduction

Since the Education Reform Act of 1988 the largest increase in staff in schools has been the group of education support staff. This is a very diverse group and in many schools this group has grown by accretion rather than in a more planned way, where an extra member of such a group was taken on each year according to the state of that year's budget rather than in a more planned way that would have been possible if finances were more predictable. Sometimes such increases have been at the expense of teaching staff, where the budget did not allow for the retention of the previous number of teaching staff but there was a little money to ameliorate the loss. In other cases it was an increase to take on a specified function to relieve pressure on teachers.

Teaching support staff are an essential group in schools at present, and most predictions suggest that schools will become more reliant on such groups in the future. A combination of pressures such as insufficient finance combined with the difficulties of recruiting teachers is likely to increase the use of teaching auxiliaries in the classroom, and also for freeing teachers from tasks outside the classroom which do not require a professional teacher to carry them out. Thus such staff are not peripheral to the work of schools, but are an increasingly vital part of it. However, national requirements for school staff have tended to focus only on teachers. Thus there is an expectation of development for teachers and there are national requirements for contracts and the appraisal of teachers, but there are no such national expectations for teaching support staff. Probably the single most important improvement in the management of staff is for schools to recognise the very disparate group of teaching support staff as one which needs managing. The introduction or review of the elements of staff management for this group as suggested in Chapter 2 may be the largest single contribution to improving morale in schools.

While such a review may bring to light elements of poor performance, it will also provide the structures to begin to tackle such problems. When it is clear whose problem it is, and whether the person is equipped to deal with it, a number of vital issues will already have been clarified. There are particular areas of schools' activities where expectations and responsibilities have magnified since 1988. This is particularly true of financial management and staff management. Staff in post often took on extra responsibilities; this was done with little time to plan and also when there were few, if any, extra resources to manage the activity. As staff leave this should be used as an opportunity to plan a more coherent structure for the management of non-teaching staff in a school. A range of organisational structures to manage teaching support staff have been proposed. A shadow structure should be planned so that as key staff leave they are not individually replaced in similar posts and, instead, the opportunity is taken to move towards the planned structure.

Often such staff are part-time, have few formal qualifications, have poorly specified duties and are taken on in the first instance for a short period of time. All of these factors, combined with the relative inexperience of teaching staff in working with support staff, have a variety of implications. Teaching support staff who are directly employed by the school include such groups as:

- bursar and finance clerks

- school secretary and office staff (including reception and telephone)
- laboratory and other technicians, including those responsible for reprographics
- site controllers, including caretaking and possibly cleaning staff
- lunchtime supervisors
- classroom and special needs assistants

There has also been an increase in staff not directly employed by the school but providing a service on a contract who may be on site for part of the day:

- those providing school meals
- grounds maintenance staff
- cleaning staff

This second group will not be covered in more detail as they are not direct employees, although evidence of poor performance of the service may need to be brought to the attention of the contractor so that they can take action.

There are in addition, and particularly in primary schools, many voluntary helpers in schools, such as parents. Some issues concerning the performance of this group may be similar to that of classroom assistants, with the major difference being that they are not paid and do not generally have a formal contract or job description.

General issues

Since this is a rapidly expanding group which is now more visible in the staffing of schools, most of the advice about poor performance will suggest that staff management practices as a whole need to be put in place for this group more than any other. This both prevents poor performance in the future and provides a structure to deal with any current poor performance. The issues involved include:

Variety of formal qualifications and experience

Compared with teachers who all have similar qualifications and some training in common, teaching support staff are much more varied. There is variety between different groups and variety within groups. It is possible to have classroom assistants who are qualified teachers working side by side with those who have no formal qualifications.

Part-time and at low cost, so less emphasis on formal staff management procedures

It often seems that because this group of workers are at the fringes of classroom activity there is less emphasis on formal staff management procedures: selection, induction, development, and so on. While on a naive cost–benefit calculation it may not seem worth putting much effort in, if things go wrong, a similar amount of senior staff time may be needed to deal with a problem performer in this group as for a teacher, and so it is false economy not to set up such posts properly in the first place. Good management is also likely to yield greater benefits from such staff for the school in terms of a better directed and higher quality service to teachers and children.

Taken on for a short fixed period which gets extended and extended

A further reason why such posts may be seen as less of an issue compared with teaching posts is that some groups, particularly special needs assistants, are taken on for short fixed periods for a particular child. This period is often either extended or is transferred to another child. Thus there may be continuity of employment but in different jobs. In its turn, this brings in additional entitlements under employment law.

Unclear job requirements

Often for many of the newer posts little is made explicit other than that the post is to help support teachers in some sort of general way. Where this is left to teachers to sort out, as in the duties of classroom assistants, this often results in such assistants providing very different forms of help in different classrooms. This can cause much resentment from those assistants who find themselves doing tasks which are unappealing while other assistants appear to have much more interesting jobs without any obvious reasons for such arbitrary differences.

Failure to consider the motivation of such employees

Although teachers may not be regarded as well paid, the pay for most support staff is much worse. The pay is not generally the main consideration for such employees. Most could earn more in other employment and so it is the total 'job package' which is important to such staff. It is features such as working hours, appreciation and recognition, and any intrinsic motivation which are important. Unless motivating factors for individuals are investigated there may be mismatches between what the individual employee finds rewarding and the nature of the job. For example, classroom assistants in one school gave helping children to learn as their major motivation, but many spent their time doing minor tasks, such as washing paint pots, which assisted the teacher, rather than working directly with children. This is not to suggest that this group should do only work which they personally find rewarding, but to suggest that there needs to be a balance that includes some work that they find rewarding if they are to be discouraged from moving to better-paid jobs.

Poor management structures

Often such staff are taken on without a clear analytical look at who will manage them and how other aspects of staff management will apply. Furthermore, such staff are often in matrix structures, more or less explicitly, and it may be unclear to whom they are responsible and for what; there may be no one in overall charge of non-teaching staff, which leaves such staff with an overall lack of corporate identity and coherence. Where there is such a person, the role may be more titular than one of active responsibility. In one secondary school, such staff chose to adopt a particular coloured overall as a way of indicating a corporate identity.

Some evidence suggests that this group is self-perpetuating. Vacancies are filled by word of mouth from existing employees rather than as a result of formal advertisements alone. If this group is not managed, it leaves a culture to build up on its own, and it is a matter of luck whether this will be conducive to school performance.

Lack of training for support staff

Until fairly recently, there have been no earmarked resources for the development of teaching-support staff and few training courses. A combination of the small number of suitable courses for groups of staff and a failure to consider the importance of training for such staff has led to little planned development of members of this group. There are now some training courses available, and NVQ certification is more prevalent. In addition to external courses, in-house training activities for groups of staff can yield worthwhile dividends. One junior school with a relatively large number of classroom assistants operated an in-house training programme led by the headteacher. This used specially adapted distance learning materials and was able to cover such sensitive subjects as confidentiality. In this way, all classroom assistants were introduced to important topics not normally discussed in the course of the day; one assistant for whom this was an issue, but who was also a school governor, could be included in a low-key way. Such courses can lead to a great increase in self-esteem and motivation if staff have never had training provided for them before.

Many schools which have taken part in Investors in People (IIP) have reported that the largest impact of such programmes is the effect on the non-teaching staff. For the first time, they have been recognised as essential members of the school community with a clear part to play in the fulfilment of the school's aims. After a school went into IIP, the attitude of the care-taker changed dramatically after taking part in staff training activities and seeing that he had an important role to play in the corporate life of the school. He became quite solicitous in finding out how he could help teachers. A primary school has developed a culture in which all teaching and teaching support staff are involved in accredited courses. Teaching support staff are involved in NVQ level 4 activities, and one is taking a degree in education.

Lack of training or preparation of teaching staff to work with and manage such staff

While there has been little training of teaching support staff, there has generally been even less thought given to the preparation of teaching staff to manage this increasing group of staff. It has often not been recognised that teaching staff need preparation and training if they are to supervise and manage such staff who work directly in their classrooms. The rise in the number of parental helpers and classroom assistants in primary classrooms has generally happened without any consideration being given as to whether teachers are equipped to organise all these other disparate sources of help. Thus classroom assistants can be carrying out very different roles in different classrooms. This can cause resentment if classroom assistants are permanently assigned to one teacher and can cause much confusion and maladaptation if classroom assistants spend part of the day with a number of teachers, all of whom have different requirements and where there is little time to communicate these requirements.

Multiple roles and members of the community, including governing body

In many schools the same member of non-teaching staff plays several different roles in the same school. A person may be a special needs assistant for part of their time, a classroom assistant for another part, and a lunchtime controller as well. Such a person is almost certainly a member of the local community; they may well be a parent or a former parent and they could even be a current or former school governor. Such a variety of relationships with a school calls for very sophisticated role switching. Sometimes problems occur because this has not been recognised. More consideration of such potential problems and how well the individuals are likely to be able to deal with such issues should be considerations when they are being appointed and developed.

eg breaks.

Poor performance

Poor performance in this group is likely to bring to light a wider range of issues than with teaching staff. These include:

- recognising poor performance
- responsibility for poor performance
- clarifying the job
- training and development for the job

Recognising poor performance

Most of the formal mechanisms by which much poor performance of teaching staff comes to light – appraisal, OFSTED school inspections, exam results, parental complaints – will be largely absent for teaching support staff. Thus, recognising poor performance will be more difficult. More general perceptions that some area of activity is not going well or that there is a difficult person in a particular post are more likely to be starting points.

Case study: Differences of view about performance

A special needs assistant (SNA) was appointed to work with pupils with statements. This seemed to work well. The SNA was very flexible about the hours she worked. She became very close to pupils, often visiting them at home or inviting them for tea. She gradually followed the SENCO's guidelines less and less. This was problematic because although the SENCO did not think she was doing a good job, parents thought she was wonderful, although this may have been because of her care and interest rather than any educational progress which the children made. Rather than confront this problem directly, the withdrawal programme was restructured which made the SNA's timetable inconvenient. She eventually left because the job was no longer worth the time it was taking.

This treatment of the SNA might have been interpreted as constructive dismissal. The alternative and much more lengthy procedure would have been to work on parental attitudes to the SNA, to have provided training and closer supervision. If this was unsuccessful, dismissal could have followed.

Responsibility for poor performance

Considering this issue may expose a lack of clarity about the details of the job, performance standards and whose responsibility it is to investigate and tackle the problem. Without adequate management structures, most of these issues are likely to fall to the headteacher. While this may be inevitable in the short term, this should lead to a resolve to formulate structures which spread the load and lead to management which is closer to the employee than the headteacher. However, if the load is to be spread this will involve delegation of responsibility and this in turn requires that the delegatee is properly prepared to take on the management task. Thus, some longer-term issues may be flagged by immediate problems of poor performance.

The responsible person needs to collect evidence about the performance of the suspected poor performer. Issues concerning the nature of the post and its priorities and who helps the member of staff decide on priorities may be highlighted. A *de facto* manager needs to be identified to 'own' the problem. The first stage should involve investigating and clarifying the work involved in the job and the performance achieved. This may yield a mismatch between the jobholder's view of the nature and importance of different aspects of their work and that which the school takes.

Case study: pitfalls of tightening up

The library assistant at a secondary school was well established in post. Although not a trained librarian, she had set up the library herself. This used a personal classification scheme which created a need for pupils to consult her in order to use the library. She had developed this role into being a listening ear for children's problems. A new headteacher tried to tighten up by:

- rewriting job descriptions of all support staff
- introducing line management with a senior manager in charge of the library assistant
- tightening up on salary differentiation and rationale for support staff
- clarifying working hours and times

The library assistant resigned and claimed constructive dismissal. The headteacher was taken to an industrial tribunal. Even though her actions were vindicated, the head felt she had been on trial.

In this case the headteacher appears to have followed the recommended procedures of tightening up for all support staff so that they were clear about expectations. But for someone who had operated in her own way for so long and was so well established in the community, such a change was unpalatable. Could anything else have been done to prevent the industrial tribunal?

Clarifying the job

The clarification of responsibilities may throw up a lack of specific skills. Training and coaching may be needed to plug this gap. There may be difficulties here, as training courses are likely to be few and unlikely to include the particular mix of skills required in a very individualised job. The relevance of training to the particular job may also need clarifying with the employee. If all of this falls to the headteacher, the time requirements begin to escalate.

Case study: recognising limitations

An administrative assistant in charge of finance was upgraded to be finance officer on the introduction of local management of schools (LMS). She had been efficient at keeping records of capitation spending, petty cash, school fund and school visits accounts. In the early days of LMS she was able to keep records of spending, but when a new administrative system was introduced and she was expected to produce plans of future spending and work more proactively, things began to go wrong. Errors began to appear in spreadsheets and she worked very long hours trying to keep up. Figures were promised but often were not forthcoming. The head reorganised duties to overcome the problem. A deputy head took charge of finance and the head became the line manager for all non-teaching staff. This continued until the finance officer retired.

This was a very expensive and inefficient solution to the problem. The basic mistake was to upgrade the existing finance officer without an adequate recognition of what might be required of such a post in the future and an adequate appreciation of whether the person could respond. One possibility would have been to make the post temporary until its future requirements were clear. This would have left scope for a better assessment of the fit between the finance officer and the new post.

Training and development for the job

There has been a general upgrading of the expectations of what office staff in particular can be expected to undertake. Few jobs do not require computer literacy. Most office staff have readily adapted their keyboard skills to computers, but a few have been left behind. Such staff should be offered training to equip them with increasingly required skills, and they should be warned that failure to upgrade their skills will, in the longer term, lead to the redundancy of their post or a dismissal for a lack of competence in the skills which are now a general requirement of all such posts.

New technology as it appears, and new requirements within an existing post, should be assumed to need training and development. Many teaching support staff do not have as high a level of intellectual ability as teachers and thus should be assumed to be less able to use generalised skills to find out any new requirements of their jobs. There may be many exceptions to this, but it is an unreasonable expectation that those on low-paid jobs should find their own solutions to problems in ways which more highly educated individuals might.

With these provisos, the general framework from earlier sections of this book for investigating, clarifying, training and developing, and supervising should be used to deal with poor performance in this group as for teachers.

Part III

Chapter 9

Case studies

INTRODUCTION

This section is made up of a series of case studies based on actual events, illustrating a variety of scenarios and possible outcomes. Two cases are described in detail to show the reality of working through capability procedures, in both cases from the headteacher's point of view. Other cases are dealt with much more briefly and from different perspectives. They are usually accompanied by commentaries or questions aimed at exploring how cases could have taken a different direction if, for example, the new procedures and expectations for dealing with lack of capability had been in operation or the culture of the particular school and management style of its leaders had been different.

The aim of this section is primarily to provide authentic illustrations of points made earlier in the book, but placed in their context and emphasising the complexity that is inevitable when dealing with the lives of fellow human beings. It is also intended that these case studies could be used as a basis for discussion or reflection to help senior managers or governors gain a greater understanding of the causes, and management, of poor performance.

CASE STUDIES

A   Detailed studies of working through the complete process of capability procedures:

    1   Jim, school caretaker – problem of capability and discipline. Took employers to industrial tribunal for wrongful dismissal.

    2   Philippa, head of art – poor performance as classroom teacher and as manager.

B   Complex cases with multiple causes and different solutions:

3   Max, head of pastoral care – role changed beyond his capacity to adapt.
4   Graham, senior manager in a primary school, weaknesses pinpointed by OFSTED.
5   George, a history teacher with both professional and personal difficulties.

C   Case in which a change of role solved a problem:

6   Wynn, head of PE, effective as teacher but not as manager.

D   A failing department:

7   A modern languages department in a middle school.

E   A temporary problem:

8   Jane, year co-ordinator in a primary school – change of membership of team caused temporary dip in performance.

F   A mismatch of personality and school culture:

9   Marcus, joining teaching after a career in the army.

G   Unresolved problems:

10 Steve, head of art – difficulty of taking over post in new school after retirement of long-established teacher.
11 Head of department in a large faculty – questions about management skills.

H   A member of staff who is not a teacher – escalating demands of the job:

12 Maureen, school receptionist.

Detailed studies of working through the complete process of capability procedures

Jim, school caretaker

This case study illustrates the difficulties of working with poor performance of a non-teaching member of staff and the tenacity and patience required of the head in following procedures through, eventually to an industrial tribunal. A principled and humane headteacher will be continually aware of the potential distress and disruption to the family should the holder of a residential post be dismissed. In such a case, it is even more difficult to maintain the confidence that the action embarked upon is the right one and to retain other stakeholders' confidence throughout the process. In this particular diocese, capability and disciplinary procedures are not enacted separately; elsewhere a choice may have had to be made, as this case has strong evidence of both incapability and misconduct.

When Sarah took over the headship of a newly created church-aided primary school on the outskirts of a medium sized town in the Midlands, she was faced with a large number of problems needing immediate solutions. The new school was the result of the merger of an infants and a junior school on the same site. They had previously been totally autonomous and with very different cultures.

Although the area included new developments with many young families moving into the area, the schools' rolls had been slowly decreasing. Both schools' headteachers has been in post for a long time and were reaching retirement age when the decision was made to amalgamate the two schools. When one head left, the deputy took over as acting head and was almost immediately appointed to a permanent headship elsewhere. An acting head was drafted in. Meanwhile, a similar scenario was being enacted in the other school, with the result that by the time the amalgamation took place most of the senior management positions were held by new people on temporary contracts.

All these changes had a very detrimental effect on morale in both schools, and the resultant drifting away of pupils only served to make the situation worse. In the meantime the quality of the environment had been steadily declining: successive acting headteachers had been much too busy with other priorities to monitor the work of the caretaker, and teachers had taken to doing general maintenance themselves, or even using the services of members of their families, because they had given up hoping that these jobs would be done by the caretaker. Nobody had taken formal action against Jim, the caretaker, up to the arrival of the eventual headteacher, Sarah, even though one of the earlier acting heads had discovered discrepancies in his overtime claims: he had been claiming for the same hours of work in both schools.

Sarah found the school to be in a desperate state. The premises had been enormously neglected, particularly the junior section of the building. The caretaker had been able to get away not only with not carrying out his caretaking duties but also with fraud because the long-standing heads of the two schools had been overwhelmed by the massive changes in their roles and could not face taking on something potentially as serious as this. The temporary post-holders subsequently had more immediate problems to deal with, and were unlikely to be in post long enough to see through formal action on this front.

Sarah's first priority was to raise morale, so she immediately set about getting the premises looking good, rearranging offices, redecorating where necessary and generally improving the state of the buildings. She soon found Jim lacked the skills and training to carry out many of these tasks and was unwilling to commit himself to reaching the standards she expected. It was not long before she and the caretaker began to clash. An added complication was that Jim was also as a popular figure in the parish, pleasant and gentle, someone who would not hesitate to do favours for anyone and who had a good rapport with the children.

Simple requests from Sarah brought no result. She found that he would agree to what she was asking but then did not carry out the task. So she moved to a more formal approach, discussing what needed to be done then following this up with a letter setting out the content of the discussion and what action had been agreed. She also always added that if he found any problems in doing what was required then he should come to her and she would discuss ways forward with him.

As she was still getting no results Sarah reported all this to the governors' premises committee and brought in relevant support people from the LEA, working with them regularly to raise Jim's consciousness of what the problems were; namely, mainly questions of cleanliness and maintenance of the premises. In spite of all this, things got worse. For whatever reason, he did not seem able to fulfil a regular commitment to the required standard.

By this point Sarah was keeping a record of everything – all meetings, discussions, agreements and monitoring of the premises on a daily basis – in order to get him to see the seriousness of the situation. She was more concerned with being professional, clear and consistent in her requirements at this stage than with the possibility of needing to use this information in a formal situation at a later stage. She wanted a bright, clean school for her pupils and staff to work in and for her caretaker to work with her to achieve this.

Sarah asked the LEA team to prepare a work schedule for Jim, setting a baseline of standards required and ensuring that what she was demanding was acceptable. Prior to doing this they did an inspection of the premises which resulted in some unpleasant discoveries: they found large quantities of banned substances within easy access of the children; they found corrosive cleaning materials left open on shelves and a standard of cleanliness that was quite unacceptable. Their report was submitted to the governors, who finally realised that something needed to be done.

Jim was, in general, a popular person with the governors, but now they began to realise that many of them had experience of problems with him and that they had allowed his pleasant personality to colour their view of him, rather than accepting objectively that there were problems with his ability to carry out his job. They had also had problems with him over lettings. At this time, early into LMS, governors' financial accountability was becoming clear but it had not been there before. When changing their regulations about lettings they discovered that the caretaker had been playing the two schools off against each other, charging for time spent in one school or the other when he was not working in either. With the new finance officer all timings were officially recorded. A close look at Jim's earnings before LMS showed that he was earning far more than the average pay for the job. This alerted the governors to the potential problem.

The senior management team started doing a premises report once a month. They still found dangerous and banned substances open and within reach of the children and standards of cleanliness that were still unacceptable. At this stage the first formal hearing took place.

October 1994: first formal hearing

The panel was made up of the chairman of governors, three other governors, the headteacher, the caretaker, a representative of the National Union of Public Employees (NUPE), on behalf of the caretaker, and an LEA representative. Much of the discussion was between the headteacher and the NUPE representative.

A significant element of the problem was that Jim could never be found. The requirement that he should be on site should have meant that he was either in the school building or in the house where he lived, but he was regularly in neither. Senior managers did premises reports regularly which covered lots of things, but basically looked at cleaning and the level of maintenance. He had copies of these. These reports included the discovery of cleaning fluid in a dangerous place and glass containers of liquid paraffin and glycerine. The caretaker's room was untidy and smelly. There was a newly opened pack of bleach left where pupils could reach it, and problems with dirt everywhere.

The findings were that the governors on the panel were mindful of the difficulties caused by the refurbishment of the school on amalgamation during the previous year, but accepted that the cleaning standard was not satisfactory. A first written warning followed after the hearing.

Staff were very disaffected, had lost hope of getting anything done and were very unsympathetic towards Jim's situation. Similarly, the deputy head, who had been acting head, had experienced many problems but had not felt able to deal with them along with everything else. Sarah also contacted the other previous heads to check that it was not a personality clash between her and Jim but a real problem of incapability. They all supported her.

The governors found Jim totally intractable. It was not so much that he violently opposed what was being asked of him, but there was simply a non-response. He did not respond in any way. If he was spoken to about some issue or action he would just say 'Oh, yes, fine'. Sarah would say 'You do understand what I'm saying?' and he'd reply 'Oh, yes'. But nothing ever happened; requests and instructions were completely ignored.

This continued for the best part of a year, with the governors seeming to be very anxious about taking action, and Sarah very mindful of the potentially difficult situation in the parish. In the summer term she produced a very detailed report to the governors giving evidence of all the continued concerns, but it was not until just late June that a second formal hearing took place, with the same members present as at the first hearing.

This time the allegations were that Jim did not clarify the lettings and did not clean up after them, that caretaking of the school had been neglected in that he left a window open, that he did not make provision for repairing a leak that had been flooding the premises and that he had not been aware that somebody had actually entered the building one morning and had been looking for him for half an hour.

Part of this was agreed, part was not because it had not been brought in time: there was no question that the allegations were not supported but that the official timescale had not been adhered to. Sarah said that the major thing she learned from all of this was the importance of being technically accurate at all stages. She felt that the industrial tribunal in particular were not concerned with the allegations made against the person in general provided that they had been well scrutinised and a fair response had been found to them; they were interested in the fact that the procedures which had been adopted had been followed to the letter and if that was so, then they found in favour of the school. This surprised Sarah because she had thought they would be looking at the pros and cons of the case, but they did not seem at all interested in this, although they did listen to all the details of the case.

June 1995: next hearing

The allegations were that Jim had failed to check and lock an outside door, and the following week had failed to check and lock the main entrance of the infants' department, which was found still to be unlocked on the afternoon of the following day. These were found proved and Jim was given a second written warning.

Sarah found the professional objectivity of her chairman of governors very helpful. This could have been an area of great difficulty, as the chair of governors was also on the parish council and so knew Jim well in a church context.

Everything said in the hearings was carefully recorded and transcripts were kept.

February 1996: final hearing

Having opened up one Friday evening for a club, Jim had lost his keys. They were found a week later. In the meantime the school had spent £600 changing all the locks in the school. This was the second time this had happened, so Sarah suspended Jim. The allegations were that in losing the keys of the school he had seriously neglected his duty and placed the security of the school at risk, and that by his own admission he had also failed to lock a kitchen door which was discovered open. In view of the seriousness of the allegations, Jim was suspended on full pay immediately until full investigations could take place and pending the outcome of the hearing. Sarah had contacted the chairman of governors immediately. She had taken immediate action because, although Jim had lost the keys on the Friday night, he had not informed her of this until the following Monday; the school had been vulnerable all weekend. She felt this merited serious action.

There was no deputy caretaker, so Sarah had to take on the responsibility of locking up herself and ended up doing so for nearly a year. This created a huge extra workload for her, but she felt it was worth it because it countered the possible accusation that she only wanted to dismiss the caretaker because she did not like Jim personally. She wanted to create some space before appointing someone new to the school. There was some newspaper coverage that was difficult for Sarah to deal with. Because of the confidential nature of the capability and disciplinary procedures, Sarah was not able to defend her position and had to endure some hostility on the part of some parishioners. She also found it difficult to reconcile her position as a manager demanding a certain standard of her employees with that of headteacher of a Christian school when she was seen as putting a committed member of the local church community out of work and out of his home.

It was an extremely stressful time, coinciding with trying to raise morale and standards in all areas of the new school and the announcement that they were to have an inspection. Sarah found it absolutely horrendous. The governors were very supportive of Sarah as were the staff. Her success was such that the inspection report was very positive and the school now figures highly in league tables.

The final hearing resulted in Jim's dismissal. However, he decided to take them to industrial tribunal, alleging wrongful dismissal. The employers offered to settle for £3,000, basically the cost of going to tribunal. Jim refused this and ended up with nothing. The tribunal found against him and stated that they found Sarah's team to have been very fair employers as they had gone through four hearings, giving him an enormous number of chances. The positive feedback and outcome for the school was not reported in the press.

The complications brought about by evidence of behaviour meriting disciplinary measures as well as lack of capability made this case particularly difficult to work through. Some authorities insist that capability and disciplinary issues are dealt with separately – capability to be tested by target setting and support to help overcome inadequacies, and disciplinary issues responded to by means of warnings and sanctions to avoid repetition of the same unacceptable incident or behaviour. Sometimes it is clear which is being dealt with, but in cases like this one the two are closely interwoven, with incapability leading to contravention of regulations or neglect of duty. Legally, it is likely that the case could have been dealt with far more quickly as some of the disciplinary offences were very serious, but headteachers need to be seen to behave fairly, morally and humanely, especially in the context of a church school. The complications brought into play by the close involvement of the local community in the life of the school led the head to ensure that every possible measure was taken to enable a positive outcome to the case. Although it was a traumatic and time-consuming period, Sarah feels she would have no hesitation in repeating the process if she felt circumstances required it, but she would see that the whole process was dealt with much more quickly now she has experience of it. A problem for many headteachers is that they are almost always novices when embarking on these procedures. They are pitted against representatives of poor performers who deal with such cases professionally on a regular basis and they do not know the likely outcomes of any action they may take.

Several heads interviewed felt very strongly that new compulsory training for headteachers should contain an input to help them deal with these processes.

Philippa, head of art

Before taking up his post as head of a small rural comprehensive, Mike was invited to take part in the appointment of a head of art. He was uneasy about the choice made, finding the teacher's portfolio of pupils' work uninspiring but not feeling confident about disagreeing with the incumbent head and chair of governors, especially as the new art teacher came from another county with excellent references from both her previous head and from the subject advisor.

Mike's unease was not dispelled by Philippa's performance in post, but at first he put this down to lack of confidence and assumed that, as she became part of the staff team, her work would improve. Mike also had a lot of other priorities. In 1991, however, the situation was brought to a head by the visit of an HMI, who stated that she found Philippa's 'organisation skills, lesson planning and preparation to be totally lacking'. Her room was a 'tip' and 'disgrace', she was not pulling her weight as a member of the department, the children received no stimulus, there was no celebration of the pupils' work, and she was only a 'good mate' in that she would do the work for the pupils. The HMI found examples of unsafe working practice. She felt Philippa was 'in need of some kind of support, that she was a big problem and her work was only appropriate to a main scale teacher'.

Mike immediately arranged a meeting with Philippa to make her aware that there were serious concerns and to inform her that formal procedures could follow. A local advisor came in to spend a day with Philippa, to get a view of how serious the situation actually was and to work with Philippa and Mike to deal with any problems that did indeed seem to exist. He found:

- Philippa had marked no work in nearly a whole term
- she left the studio unattended
- she allowed the use of sharp knives without a safety ruler
- she had no lesson plans
- nor did she have any teacher's notes
- there was litter left on the floor
- there were no schemes of work or planning documentation

This was confirmed in a letter to Philippa, inviting her to show her ability to work acceptably in another observed lesson the following week. Although she did respond to many of the issues, there were still several areas of concern and a further meeting was arranged.

It then became difficult to arrange this second meeting: the letter from the head went astray, then Philippa said she did not have time to prepare for the meeting and suggested a date and time that would be convenient for her and her 'friend' that then had to be agreed with Mike. Mike took advice from his LEA personnel department, who were unwilling to move quickly towards formal procedures, emphasising the importance of adequate time and support before agreeing to set about the formal process.

In view of this and in order to minimise the effect on pupils, Mike reorganised the curriculum area by appointing a head of creative arts and making Philippa in charge of art within this faculty.

By January 1992 there had still been no appreciable improvement, so Mike invoked the LEA's assistance procedures for teachers experiencing professional difficulties, commencing with the informal stage as in the authority's procedures. The expectation was that by the end of May targets would be met. These targets were based on safety procedures, marking, planning and standards. The relevant LEA advisor would monitor this and at the end of the summer term another meeting would take place, at which the situation would be assessed and decisions would be made as to whether capability or disciplinary procedures would follow.

There were also concerns about stock checking and incomplete records of achievement. A great deal of anxiety and extra work for other colleagues was caused because the personal statements of pupils in Philippa's form were not available when the deadline for them arrived.

In April 1992, an advisory teacher observed a lesson with the same class as seen earlier by the subject inspector. She found that planning and organisation were still a problem, the lesson was late starting because resources were not properly organised, and so on. The head of creative arts taught art and knew the standard of Philippa's work. The rest of the department was very concerned about standards of work and especially about safety in the studios.

Another meeting in July with the inspector (following another lesson observation) reinforced this view. Although some progress had been made – orderly beginning to lesson, register called – the main areas had not been solved. Safety procedures were still not followed, marking was still not systematic, planning was haphazard. The inspector suggested that assistance and support continue with another meeting in October.

Philippa refused to consent to another meeting until she had consulted her legal advisor. She felt the head's and inspector's conduct had been unprofessional. She said she did not have time to seek advice until after the start of the autumn term. The meeting eventually took place early in November.

By February 1993 there seemed to be a substantial improvement and it was agreed, after a final lesson observation by the inspector, that informal procedures should be concluded. Mike breathed a sigh of relief and turned his mind to other issues.

The school had an OFSTED inspection in February 1994. Philippa was only observed twice, neither time by a subject specialist, and deemed satisfactory (as far as could be deduced from the report). But by December two years later, serious concerns about Philippa's work had arisen again.

The next episode highlights the difficulties that can ensue if people offer help informally! An advisory teacher helping install new equipment saw Philippa teaching and suggested to Mike that, as he had known Philippa for many years, he could have an informal chat with her about perceived problems. Philippa's response to this was to make a formal complaint to the chairman of governors about the head's unprofessional behaviour in discussing concerns about a colleague with a 'peer' without firstly telling her (Philippa) about this. It transpired that Philippa and the advisory teacher had trained together. The head's response was that he would expect to discuss with advisory teachers the work of relevant colleagues. The complaint was not pursued further but all the problems that gave rise to concerns about safety, standards and planning were once again apparent in Philippa's work.

So in March 1996 Mike found himself restarting the informal stage of the formal capability procedures. With the inspector (now called an advisor) he compiled a list of ten required outcomes. These were that:

1   units of work be properly planned
2   work be regularly marked
3   suitable supplies be ordered for the department
4   health and safety issues be dealt with properly

5   work be set during absences unless this is not reasonable
6   Philippa be on time for lessons
7   studios and the department office be properly organised
8   pupils' work be completed so they have a finished project in which they can take pride at the end of the module
9   in the long term examination results improve
10 there be improved liaison with colleagues

Philippa made a long response to these points, either refuting them or defending her position. A further response from the head of faculty supported the requirements.

In June 1996 a meeting confirmed that the targets had not been met, but Philippa asserted that they had not been reasonable: some were not clear enough and others unmeasurable, especially the last two. So a new set of targets was drafted, indicating precisely what needed to be done, what support would be given to enable paperwork and so on (planning, schemes of work) to be in place by September when formal proceedings would otherwise start.

Every Thursday after school a member of the senior management team (a senior teacher) and the head of faculty would be available to provide support for Philippa on any issue whatsoever. A deputy head would be responsible for collecting evidence.

In spite of all this, Philippa failed to turn up for invigilation and missed deadlines. She never took the opportunity to attend the proposed Thursday support meetings.

A review meeting was held in October to keep things on track. Some targets were being met, others were still to be completed. Throughout all this Philippa was uncommunicative: she gave no indication to anyone involved in the process of how she felt about what was happening, and only spoke at meetings to confirm that she heard and understood what was agreed. Mike felt that Philippa felt that she was being unjustly persecuted, but he had no evidence of this and it could well have been Mike's own anxiety about the effect he was having that gave him this feeling. Philippa was in her late forties and had a young family. It was not without realising the potentially serious effect on Philippa's family that Mike continued to pursue the course that he felt to be right. It was the standards Philippa achieved professionally that were the issue.

December 1996 marked the end of Stage 1 of the formal proceedings. Many targets had not been met. Mike was not satisfied, and therefore proposed beginning Stage 2. The targets remained unaltered but were further refined so that there was no doubt about any meaning or requirement. The county advisor also went through these targets with Philippa to ensure that everyone had the same understanding of what was required.

Under the regulations as they existed at that point, Stage 2 required a full term to enable progress and monitoring, so the review meeting would take place at the end of February. Before this happened, the other teacher in the department sent a letter of complaint to the head of faculty about Philippa.

The final meeting took place just after Easter. Mike confirmed that targets had not been met and he would be seeking Philippa's dismissal. The representative of Philippa's professional association made it clear that he felt there was nothing that Philippa could defend and he would recommend that she resign. A date was set for the meeting with the governors (Stage 3 of formal proceedings) in May. Philippa tendered her resignation on the eve of this meeting. After this she formally complained to the chair of governors about the treatment she had received, saying that she had no evidence of some of the issues that had been used against her and wished these to be clarified. The chair of governors was advised by the LEA how to respond to this, knowing that procedures had been correctly followed.

Philippa now has a post in an independent school.

The success of the situation from the headteacher's point of view was greatly helped by the quality of support from the deputy head and the head of faculty. The dissatisfaction of the other member of department and the change in climate concerning dismissal of staff led to the second attempt succeeding where the first attempt had been abortive. At first, both governors and the LEA had been very unwilling to embark on the formal capability procedure: they were both unsure of the likely response from other stakeholders (such as staff and parents) and of the likelihood of achieving a successful outcome (a sustained improvement in performance would have been seen as a successful outcome – the teacher's dismissal was not the aim of the exercise).

Complex cases with multiple causes and different solutions

Max

This case explores what happens when the role to which a teacher was appointed has changed beyond his capability to adapt. There are also issues about changing culture in a school over the years and the ensuing changes in expectations. There were several different possible outcomes to this case which are explored at the end.

Max had been appointed to a head of first year post when the school was established as a mixed comprehensive in the early 1970s. Acutely falling rolls led to a cut in posts and to Max taking over responsibility for pastoral care in the school. He knew the pupils (some 450) and their parents very well, having met them all on entry into the school, and developed an easy, informal relationship with them. He was quite happy to ring parents in the evenings or at weekends, and even dropped in on them if there was some concern about their children that he wanted to discuss with them. All discipline problems were dealt with by him (there were rumours that he was very effective at using a ruler as a deterrent!) and distressed children found a comforting arm around them.

The year heads had little more than an administrative function (checking registers and arranging meetings); when they wished for a more active role they found it difficult because both pupils and parents automatically went directly to Max. He made some effort to involve year heads, but his style was not really delegatory and he constantly dealt with problems himself rather than referring them to the relevant year head.

By the early 1990s and the arrival of a new headteacher, the school roll had increased and Max had been promoted to a senior teacher post in recognition of this. However, it became more and more difficult for Max to deal with everything by himself. Furthermore, his manner with pupils was felt to be inappropriate on occasions. A large number of parents and pupils felt that he was a sort of 'uncle' figure and were very fond of him, but a growing number were beginning to express unease about his tendency to put his arm round girls who seemed distressed and his practice of tweaking the ear of any boy whose behaviour was not quite right. He was also showing great signs of stress as he rushed from one crisis to another, trying to deal with every problem in the school.

There were many changes in the requirements of his job. He was no longer required to be a father figure to the pupils in the school. He was supposed to be leading a team of year heads, supporting them while they dealt with much of the work that he had been doing. But, much more importantly, the role of pastoral care within the school was changing from being predominantly concerned with day-to-day problems to being more preventative and developmental. Max was unable to adapt to this. He did not understand the new role, he did not approve of it and he had no intention of changing from a style which he found personally gratifying. He had evidence of the success of his interpretation of the role in the number of ex-pupils who came back especially to see him years after they had moved on. He was also supported by some of the year heads, who had been brought up in the role as he had decreed it. They lacked confidence in their own ability to fulfil the new role so allied themselves closely to him.

The new head knew that the pastoral system would break down if necessary changes were not made. There were now over 800 pupils in the school, so even from the most practical point of view it was obvious that one person could not deal with everything that happened. A minimum of delegation was needed just to make the job possible. If the nature of the role was also to change it was going to be necessary to change Max's attitude or for someone else to take charge of the pastoral system.

There were several possible ways forward. The first was to persuade Max to change his style and to participate in the training necessary to enable him to lead those involved in implementing appropriate changes. Max, perhaps fearful that he might not succeed or perhaps genuinely not understanding the new demands on him, dug his heels in. He attended a couple of days INSET on the changing role of pastoral care, but there was no evidence of any change in his practice as a result of this. The second way forward was to appoint someone else to manage the changes. This would be possible by changing the roles of the two deputy heads. The current situation was that Max was responsible for pastoral care, and the deputies took responsibility for the curriculum and for administration. The new head had been looking for ways to recast these roles to allow for more flexibility, but had had no opportunity to do so. Unfortunately, unless one of the deputies retired, the opportunity was still not available. The third possibility was to find a different but equally acceptable role for Max. The possibilities at senior teacher level were staff development and finance. The head hoped the former would appeal because of the direct working with colleagues, the 'up front' status and the opportunity to develop the role as he wished (to a large extent). The second possibility was more risky considering Max's qualifications and experience, but the school needed someone to work on implementing the new computerised financial package, to make presentations to governors about the state of the budget and to prepare budget forecasts. On the surface this very much appealed to Max, so a change of role was agreed. Unfortunately, he soon found that he missed the close relationships he had had with parents and pupils and began to be less and less motivated to succeed in his new role. His support group of 'old' year heads had also disappeared as colleagues adapted to the new style of leadership: they actually preferred having more responsibility once they were enabled to take it on, and some felt some resentment towards Max for not having helped them develop the skills they needed. Gradually he became less and less effective, and when the opportunity came to volunteer for redundancy he took it.

Convenient opportunities to take early retirement or to volunteer for redundancy are not always available, nor are the possibilities of complete changes of role. There are two points at which this case could have taken the teacher down the capability route. The first was when he was given INSET opportunities to update his skills but showed no evidence of changing his working style as a result of this. Substantial evidence of his failure to carry out his revised role as the person responsible for pastoral care had already been collected, along with evidence of the support and training put in place to help him update his skills as required. If the headteacher had decided on this route at this stage it would have been quite reasonable, but it would also have been a difficult and stressful time for many people. Max was well known to many people involved at some point with the school, and still had supporters among the staff, governors and parents who would have influenced the case emotionally.

The second time when capability procedures might have been started was when Max began to be less effective in his new role. There was already evidence of a great deal of support being given to enable him to change roles, and to this was gradually being added a body of evidence of poor performance in a second post in the school. By this time the capability route would have had less impact on the wider community of the school; Max's staff supporters had themselves changed their view of the pastoral role and his supporters among the governors had now seen the effects of poor performance in a role that affected them more closely.

It is one of the less attractive aspects of school improvement that leads to staff who were once seen to be highly successful being removed because the expectations of their role have changed. Sometimes they do not agree with the changes, feeling perhaps that these take them further away from direct contact with pupils, and often this resistance eventually affects their ability to make the changes necessary for them to fulfil the new role.

Graham

In this case study there are a range of complex issues: the teacher concerned is a senior manager, an experienced and well-established member of staff and well-known as part of the local community. Since his appointment, however, both the requirements and expectations of his role have changed substantially and there is some doubt about his ability to make the changes needed for success. An OFSTED inspection pinpointed this problem, amongst others, and a new headteacher was appointed to deliver the post-OFSTED action plan.

Karen took up her post as head of a large primary school in January 1996 three months after an OFSTED inspection. The previous head having left at the end of the previous term, the deputy had been acting head for the autumn term. Karen's appointment took place just before the inspection, so she was able to work with the deputy and governors immediately to see the implications of the inspection findings and to devise an action plan.

The inspection report was not enthusiastic about the levels of achievement in the school, and particularly questioned the quality of teaching and learning in the classes of three of the very experienced teachers on Karen's staff, two of whom decided to take early retirement at the end of that year. The third had been absent during much of the week of the inspection.

On the surface there were no unexpected problems. The school staff were very stable and experienced: five teachers had been in the school some twenty-five years each, two had been there about seven years and the five new teachers had been appointed as staff retired and numbers of classes increased as the roll grew. Many of the parents had been pupils themselves at the school, had been taught by the same teachers and had an understandable loyalty and affection for them. There were no discipline problems; pupils were polite and biddable. The atmosphere in the school was warm and friendly.

The OFSTED inspection, however, showed up inconsistencies of expectations between classes and a general lack of teamwork and co-ordination, leading to signs of considerable underachievement in some curriculum areas across the school and in most areas in Graham's class. Karen's first priority would be to clarify the roles of subject co-ordinators and set up systems to enable teams to work on schemes of work and so on. Graham, the teacher causing concern, was maths co-ordinator as well as head of years 3 and 4, and as such was a member of the senior management team. He had not produced any schemes of work, nor any materials to promote maths in the school. Along with the other older members of staff, he had been used to working autonomously, using his experience to decide which bits of the syllabus he would cover and how. After the inspection, the other older teachers understood the need for collaboration and planning: one decided she did not want the workload this required, so retired. The second made a great effort to take on the new way of working, was delighted with the positive effects of sharing ideas and so found a new enthusiasm for her work.

It soon became apparent that there had been previous undercurrents of discontent about Graham's work. The chair of governors' children had passed through his class and she embarrassedly confessed to Karen that she was glad when the children moved on to the next teacher, even though the children themselves had been very happy in Graham's class. The deputy head had been uneasy about the poor quality of display work in the classroom but had not felt confident to comment, thinking that this was just an area where the teacher was not talented. Some parents were unsure about the progress their children had made, but lacked the confidence to ask questions; after all, Graham had so much experience.

In order to raise standards generally and to ensure that the pupils in Graham's class received the same curriculum as in other classes, Karen decided to prioritise English and classroom environment. The English co-ordinator was very competent, and so would set a good standard for other co-ordinators to follow as their subject became the priority. All would be very open and shared.

It soon became clear that, for whatever reason, Graham was not taking his share in the work. His planning consisted of descriptions of tasks rather than learning objectives or evaluation. Karen provided INSET and worked individually with him to build up these skills. Graham eventually conceded that he was finding it all too much and began to take time off with stress-related illnesses. The post-OFSTED check carried out by advisors found deficiencies in Graham's paperwork and commented on low expectations of standards of work in his class. They also criticised the maths documentation. Graham said he had not wanted the co-ordinator role: it was too much along with all the other work he was expected to do.

Then began a regular series of meetings where Karen and Graham looked at possible ways out of this problem. He asked for a year off to gain different experiences. The governors refused this. He asked to drop his SMT role; the governors agreed. He asked to co-ordinate a different year group, but governors refused. It was eventually agreed that he should take over the co-ordination of PE. This raised issues regarding Graham's salary: he was no longer a member of senior management and was now responsible for a less significant curriculum area in terms of planning and assessment. Historical anomalies in the pay structure in the school still prevented implementation of a clearly formulated pay policy, so Graham was not the only member of staff being paid what appeared to be a higher rate than his actual role might merit. Karen and her governors were looking to improve Graham's performance, not to demotivate him. Furthermore, Karen had not yet been able to put clearly defined job descriptions in place, so there were no benchmarks in existence linking roles with salaries in any way. Probably, therefore, it would have been impossible to argue that Graham should take a pay cut in line with the cut in responsibilities.

The new year began with the change of roles. Karen allowed time for Graham to settle into his new situation, but by half-term there was still no proper planning for PE and the work in English in his class was still at an unacceptable standard. The English co-ordinator complained that the reading corner was not being properly used, reading records were perfunctory and not developmental, and children with learning difficulties in English were not being identified.

At this point (the end of October) Karen decided she could accept the situation no longer and began the informal stage of the lack of capability procedure. All previous meetings and requirements had been documented so she was able to show Graham that her expectations had been clear and that he had not met them. At the meeting precise targets were set (for example, reading records to be completed in line with school policy, planned use of the reading corner to be documented and implemented) and the English co-ordinator was enlisted to work with Graham to meet the targets by the end of term.

This is the current position. Karen is confident about the route she is now on, but she is very concerned about the likely outcomes. Graham is himself the NUT representative in an area where the professional associations have been investigating accusations of bullying of teachers by their heads. Parents will support him through loyalty and through genuine fondness for someone who has always been in their lives. Children are fond of the avuncular teacher who always has chocolate bars in his desk drawer. Colleagues, although exasperated by his failure to carry his share of the workload, are not keen to see a long-term peer dismissed, especially as he only recently married another local teacher.

Successful schools are characterised by good relationships with all stakeholders. Karen is all too well aware of the need to balance insistence on professional standards against the possible negative effects of the human issues involved.

What is the likelihood of Graham succeeding in meeting his targets and raising the quality of his work to a standard acceptable to Karen and her governors? He has been in a poor environment – a school where standards had not been particularly high and where sharing of ideas had not been the norm. He could not have known what standards were possible and what was being achieved in the school and elsewhere. His ability as a manager had not been questioned before and expectations had not been made clear. The answer to the question is therefore complex and requires the answer to several other questions: Is he intellectually capable of raising the standard of his work? Does he have the skills to do it? And is he motivated to do it?

If the answer to the first of these is yes, then a positive result will depend on his motivation to succeed. If it is no, then it is a true case of lack of capability and Karen will be continuing through the procedures towards an eventual dismissal. If he just does not have the skills to succeed, then support and INSET should enable him to overcome this problem, providing of course he is motivated to do it. Is he motivated to do it? Only Graham has the answer to this. Does he need his salary to maintain his new lifestyle or can he now afford to find a different way forward with his new wife's support? Does he want to put his energy and time into acquiring new professional skills, or is he more interested in laying the foundations of his new relationship? It seems that the only way for him to find out the answers is in his response to Karen's decision to work through capability procedures in his case.

George

This case looks at long-standing poor performance combined with personality clashes with colleagues and a concern on the part of the school community about a member of staff's dependence on his work.

George was appointed as head of history in 1975 from another local school with good references from the head. From the earliest years in this post there had been a record of disagreements with colleagues in the department and many complaints about his leadership of the department. In 1983 there had even been a discussion with a senior LEA officer with a view to demoting him. It seems that in fact the first stage of capability procedures was being set up. His two departmental colleagues at that time had written a joint letter listing complaints ranging from the lack of schemes of work to the difficulties of day-to-day personal relationships. At different times he had joined different teachers' professional associations and, for whatever reason, had been dissatisfied with all of them. He used a private solicitor to help him respond to the complaints and, more specifically, to the manner in which the complaints were being dealt with. He countered with a grievance procedure taken out against the headteacher. No action resulted from this.

The head had very mixed feelings about George and how to deal with him. He knew that work in the history department was not of a good standard, but this was still a time when many long-term heads saw their role as benevolent despots with a responsibility to care for staff as if they were family members. He also knew that George seemed to have no friends either in or out of school, and apparently no other interests. He actually feared that George might commit suicide if too heavily pushed to improve. This was not an exaggerated fear, as George himself had even talked about this to pupils who had then anxiously passed the information on to their form teachers. Not only did he have no friends on the staff or among the pupils, bu he had no close relations. On the form he filled in when registering on the staff, he had written 'not known' in the space for next of kin. He seemed to be a very lonely man who, in spite of all appearances to the contrary, actually needed what his job in the school offered him.

The examination results of his classes had been poor for many years, but there were no discipline problems so he caused no disruption to colleagues' work. His classes in fact worked in silence while he invigilated rather than taught them. Other members of the department chose either to work autonomously, ignoring him, or to move on as quickly as possible to other posts. It had been fortunate that there was very rarely an NQT appointed to the history department and that for long periods other history teachers held other posts of responsibility in the school: they were able to work without needing George's support, and, except for the time when they collaborated to make their formal complaint against him, ignored him. Colleagues' responses to the lack of action after the complaint are not known, but it is likely that it led them to agree that ignoring him was the best course to take.

In September 1990 a new head took over and was very concerned about the consistently poor examination results: they had been the worst in the authority for the subject and the worst of all subjects in the school over three consecutive years. An advisor came to spend a day in the department and wrote a very long report in which he found concerns about every possible aspect of both George's teaching and his management of the department. (This was in October of that year.)

Soon after this George became ill, was hospitalised and had several small operations to correct digestive problems. This necessitated prolonged and frequent absences. He was absent for periods of three or four days on eleven occasions during 1991.

In January 1992 the school was inspected by the local authority. The history inspector made the following list of concerns about George's work:

- no schemes of work for the department
- no consistent homework set
- no lesson plans
- no organised or focused displays
- no inventory of equipment and resources
- no planned staff development
- no assessment procedures
- no policies
- no interaction between the teacher and pupils

In fact, there was no positive comment that she could find to make.

Knowing that he had only recently returned from sick leave, but also knowing that the problems dated from before his illness and were not caused by it, she privately discussed with George the options open to him: retirement due to ill health or probable capability procedures. By March 1992 he had retired on the grounds of ill health.

Overt staff reaction to all this was nil. George really had had no supporters or friends on the staff or among pupils, but no one wished anything bad for him; they just wanted to work at a high standard and he was hindering their progress. He has not committed suicide but is working privately.

George was fortunate that he had a choice of options available to him and was able to move out with an assured income and without being dismissed. This option is becoming less and less available. It is likely now that in a case such as George's, where there is documented evidence of poor performance over a long period of time, that the new, faster procedures could be used and George would leave quickly once the decision to begin the formal process has been made. Anxieties about how the person will cope once deprived of the work and surroundings that seemed to fulfil their needs for security and social intercourse, however limited, are obviously going to be in the back of the mind of whoever is dealing with the poor performance. Professionally, however, the pupils needs should always be paramount.

Case in which a change in role solved the problem

Wynn

This study looks at working with an experienced teacher who has certain strengths but is not succeeding in the role that his post has become. He is enabled to step down from his position of responsibility without losing face and rediscover his motivation.

Wynn was an enthusiastic rugby player. As a teenager in Swansea, he had soon earned his place in the first team and was very much in demand as coach with the juniors. He was not very academic but knew that he was talented as a teacher of rugby. His birthday was in early September. At this time (about thirty years ago) teachers were in short supply and schools were expanding rapidly, so the physical education college was prepared to take some candidates after only one year in the sixth form, provided they could show their potential as teachers. This suited Wynn ideally, so the week after his eighteenth birthday he began his Certificate in Education.

The week before his twenty-first birthday, Wynn began his first teaching job in a new comprehensive being created from a secondary modern in north London. His skill as a sports teacher was undoubted. He had surpassed all expectations, being the first member of his family to qualify to enter a profession. He was happy. In fact, he remained totally content with his life for twenty years. He married a local girl and was promoted first to head of boys PE and then to head of the physical education faculty.

Then in the early 1990s, things began to go wrong. Over forty years old, Wynn began to find days running up and down the games fields left him very tired. Also, the PE curriculum had been changing over the years. Generally this had not affected Wynn, as he stuck with rugby in the winter, cricket in the summer and left the mixed, indoor activities to the rest of the teaching team. But the school roll had a period of sharp decrease and it became necessary for many staff to be more flexible, teaching across the range of their faculty area. The headteacher, who had also been in the school for over twenty years, retired at about this time and the new head was likely to make a lot of changes.

Suddenly Wynn began to feel out of touch: he realised that he had not really been leading his faculty but allowing everyone to do what they wanted without making any plans for future development. Those who had seen what was going to happen had prepared themselves by acquiring new skills. Like many PE teachers, they sought promotion through the pastoral hierarchy or by being in at the beginning of 'new' subjects such as IT and business studies. So Wynn's team experienced great changes and Wynn was ill-prepared to lead his new team, now mainly consisting of newly qualified teachers and 'part-time' PE teachers whose main role was head of year, or staff development co-ordinator. Both groups were heavily reliant on Wynn for planning, organisation and up-to-date curriculum information.

He did not like to ask for help with this; after all, he was one of the most experienced faculty heads in the school. However, he began to suffer from lots of physical discomforts, such as problems with his back and stomach pains. He felt very guilty about it, but was forced to take a lot of time off school to see his GP and other consultants. He did not seem to link his increasing inability to do his job effectively with his increasing absenteeism. He was very conscientious and was not consciously opting out.

The deputy head responsible for the curriculum was the first person to become aware of the problem; with the advent of the first version of the national curriculum he was working with heads of faculty to create new documentation. He found that Wynn was regularly absent on days that meetings had been arranged and, when they did manage to talk, he seemed to have little idea of how he would be delivering the new curriculum. The problem therefore was escalating.

Wynn was given priority to attend all available county courses for heads of PE, but he was again hampered by health problems. The deputy head began to look at Wynn's attendance figures and discovered that he had not completed a single week since the second half of the autumn term. It was now Easter. He arranged a meeting with Wynn, who was ill on the arranged day, but they eventually succeeded in meeting and discussing Wynn's state of health. Wynn was frank about his anxieties about his health and his wish to recover his earlier fitness. He was less willing, however, to agree that his recurrent absences were having a bad effect on his pupils' progress. To a great extent his department had been covering for him, so other staff had not been needed to cover PE lessons in his absence. The main effect of his absences were on his tutor group and in his planning and development of schemes of work. Both of these were areas which would produce problems in the longer term but were having no noticeable immediate effect.

It was with the longer term in mind that the deputy head (having discussed this with the new head) arranged an appointment for Wynn with the county medical officer. His report suggested that Wynn's ill health was genuine but mainly stress-related, and that it would be a good idea to look at the demands of his particular role with a view to reducing the stressors. At first Wynn was very reluctant to agree that the situation might be the result of stress. He had very clear physical symptoms and insisted that, as soon as suitable treatment could be found, all would be well. Reluctantly, he did agree that he had fallen seriously behind in his role as head of faculty and that he would enlist the help of the PE advisor to find some strategies for catching up.

The PE advisor met first with Wynn and then with the faculty team. This was made easier by the recent confirmation that the school was to have an inspection in the early autumn and the invitation to all curriculum leaders to have their faculty 'health checked' first. Wynn had agreed with the advisor to try and share the necessary work round the department, but he found many problems as he set about doing this. The first problem was that the more senior members of the team were all team leaders in other areas, and so were unwilling to work on PE planning when they knew that their own priorities would take much of their available time. The second problem was that the remaining staff were NQTs or part-timers: the former group were willing but lacking the skills and knowledge to work without Wynn's close guidance, and the latter were not willing to take on such potentially large tasks. The third, and most serious, problem was that Wynn himself did not really understand what was actually needed, and so could not divide up the task, give clear guidance on carrying it out or monitor the team's progress.

His recent attendance on courses had not been useful in helping him gain the necessary understanding of new developments because he had not been involved in the gradual evolution of the PE curriculum. He had been unable to make sense of the new methods of assessing pupils' skills and how to create the documentation to enable his department to assess pupils' learning.

He now began to realise that he was incapable of achieving the targets he had agreed with the advisor but could see no way out of the problem. He also had a young family and so was very concerned about his financial situation, his head of department allowance being crucial. The job that he had enjoyed had changed out of all recognition; he had less contact with pupils than he would have wished, especially as the ever-increasing meetings timetable was preventing him from coaching teams after school. It seemed like a vicious circle. Then a young colleague unintentionally came up with a solution: relinquish the head of department role and use the extra time gained to build up contacts that would enable him to make up the financial deficit through coaching. When he looked in detail at his budget Wynn realised that, after tax, the allowance for his management role was not a huge amount.

The effects of this possible solution on school development were discussed and seen to be advantageous, enabling a promotion possibility for a talented colleague, a better experience for pupils in the department, and, in the longer term with continuing falling rolls, the possibility of Wynn working part-time in school as his out-of-school commitments grew. In fact, he developed a successful small business. With the pressure of managerial commitments and anxiety about his finances removed Wynn's health improved and he was able to continue to work very effectively.

This situation was solved happily for all concerned, but it depended for its success on the good will of all stakeholders. In a different establishment there might have been the feeling that it would be a good opportunity to remove an ageing PE teacher and replace him with someone younger and more dynamic. In some cases this could well have been the best solution. Also, Wynn's business endeavours could have been unsuccessful, leaving him and his family in some difficulty. Furthermore, pension legislation current at the time worked against Wynn's best interests in stepping down from his post, but new arrangements allow for teachers to opt to retain their pension entitlement at the level at which they step down from a higher paid role and top up their further payments until actually retiring. The main reason that Wynn accepted the proposition was his love of teaching and his knowledge that he actually was a good teacher. It is important that there is not an automatic assumption that a management role is 'better' than a purely teaching role and, conversely, that anyone who does not become a manager is a poor teacher.

A failing department

A modern languages department in a middle school

Not all poor performance can be attributed to an individual, wherever they may be in the management hierarchy. Sometimes the work of a whole department is not up to the required standard. This study also explores the difficulty of gathering evidence for poor performance in a middle or high school where a secondary school curriculum is followed but the pupils move on to upper schools for their GCSE courses, and therefore there are no external examination results which relate directly to their middle school work.

Jack had been delighted to be appointed to the headship of a middle school. He had always preferred working with the middle-range pupils and knew that most of the teachers in the school had positively chosen to work with this age range. But there was one area which caused him concern from the very beginning.

When Jack mentioned his anxieties about his modern languages department to colleagues at his first meeting of local heads, he found much sympathy. It is not easy to recruit modern language teachers to high or middle schools that take pupils to the age of thirteen or fourteen. The majority of language teachers are women and, once established professionally and personally, are typically likely to be less mobile geographically than men. Career-minded language teachers are, understandably, wary of taking posts in schools where there are no examination classes and, in a rural area, there are fewer teachers positively choosing to take posts away from home (because of their own family commitments, for example).

So Jack found that he was constantly recruiting linguists who stayed for a year and then moved to posts in schools offering them GCSE classes. In a small school with a very limited budget, his governors had no flexibility to try retaining particularly promising young teachers by paying them more. Even if he could have tried this it was unlikely to be a successful strategy, as experience of teaching examination classes was likely to be more valuable to them in the longer term.

Salary was also a problem as regards recruitment of a suitable head of department. The department was small: there were two full-time teachers and some part-time help depending on the availability of other staff able to teach some French and the size of the intake year. Therefore the head of department had a fairly full teaching commitment and was paid two extra points only. The present head of department had been appointed when very young, as a first promotion. She had seemed ideal as someone who would stay three or four years, improving standards and injecting life into the department, and then move on to a bigger department. It did not happen like that, and she had now been in the school fifteen years.

At first she had been exactly as hoped for, and had reinvigorated the department and the status of languages in the school. Then she had started looking for a promotion, but by now had a partner locally and, quite understandably, was not prepared to travel too far afield to work. The expected promotion never happened. She got married and years passed.

It was at this stage that Jack became head of the school. He felt the languages department to be one of the weakest in the school, but with no examination results and no Key Stage 3 assessments he had little evidence on which to base this feeling. It continued to be difficult to monitor as new recruits continued to move on. He and his governors eventually decided on a different tactic and appointed a mature trained NQT, a French national married to a local vet.

Nathalie took a while to settle in and had some early problems with classroom management and control. These seemed normal NQT problems and were gradually resolved. The languages advisor had observed lessons and found them satisfactory so Jack felt that he could now relax a little about the languages department and concentrate on preparing the school for an OFSTED inspection in the following term.

The OFSTED inspectors identified the department as weak, making it a key issue that standards be raised in that department. In their report they stated that the quality of teaching and learning should be improved, that the profile of language learning in the school should be raised and that methods of assessment in the department should be devised so that they were integral to the programme and informed teachers and learners of the progress being made.

Jack was anxious not to implement a knee-jerk reaction and was confused by the conflicting messages he had received from the local advisor and from the OFSTED inspection. He was also anxious not to destroy the confidence of the department beyond repair. On reflection, he decided that the confusion had arisen because he and the advisor had concentrated on the basic teaching skills of the NQT and had not looked at the role of the head of department, who had been known to the advisor throughout both their careers in the county. Assumptions had been made about the high quality of work continuing as it had in the first years after Nathalie took up the post: no one had really looked at progress and development while the major changes had been happening in language teaching and, more importantly, the assessment of language learning.

The two members of the languages department were in a state of shock. Nathalie had felt she had overcome her original problems, no longer having serious difficulties with classroom management or disruptive pupils. She was, however, unaware of much methodology and quite unaware of new assessment requirements. Her head of department had not worked with her on either of these areas, and her own background in France had given her no insight into possible ways of teaching in England. A great deal of work was needed with both of them.

Assuming that the OFSTED inspectors had judged the department accurately, why had such a situation developed? This was through a complex mixture of assumptions and pressures relating to the particular situation of the school:

- an assumption that the head of department had kept abreast of developments in language teaching and assessment;
- that she understood the role of head of department in relation to other members of the department beyond classroom management and control;
- a history of difficulties in recruiting good quality language teachers to this type of school led to lower expectations for the quality of teaching and learning in that department;
- a teacher who had not experienced the English education system at first-hand as a pupil and student would need to learn the methodologies practised in that system;

- it is difficult to develop good practice in a small department without outside stimulus.

Work with Nathalie began immediately, with enrolment on a course especially designed for teachers in her situation: this started with a Saturday school on methodology and then continued over five evening sessions, reinforced with focused lesson observation by a senior member of staff designated as Nathalie's mentor. She was eager to learn once she realised that the extra work was needed not because she was a poor teacher, but was intended to enable her to extend her skills and become a very effective teacher. She was also able to see how schemes of work, lesson planning and assessment could be built up together to improve pupils' learning. This was very different from her experience in France and should have been part of her learning after being appointed to the school. INSET for Nathalie and time for lesson observation and feedback were very expensive, using a large share of the staff development budget, but both Jack and Nathalie felt it to have been money well spent. The only problem now is whether Nathalie will be looking for a move to a larger school in the near future so that she can continue to develop her skills. This will probably depend on how the head of department has responded to the demands for change.

In the meantime the languages advisor has been working with the head of department to bring schemes of work up to date and to discuss the job description of a head of department. In this school there is a generic job description based on the responsibility for ensuring pupils receive their entitlement in that particular area and covering deployment of resources, curriculum planning and monitoring, attendance at relevant meetings, communication with and from the department, and so on. When more closely addressed, it was clear that the head of modern languages saw her role as no wider than deployment of resources, both human and material: she allocated a teacher and textbooks to all classes. However, she had been supportive in helping Nathalie deal with early classroom disruption, and to a limited degree, dealing with day-to-day management of the department, she was effective and the department had an atmosphere of good working relationships.

This was the role she had been inducted into nearly fifteen years previously. After the first few years her career seemed not to be progressing but her personal life passed through many stages: she was first engaged, then married, then hoping for children, then experiencing problems in her marriage and finally divorced. She had not noticed that the demands of her professional life had changed and, until the OFSTED inspection, nothing had suggested this to her. There were no benchmarks against which to measure her performance, and the constant turnover of second in department had probably served to reinforce her in her restricted role. Her inexperienced colleagues had need for support in basic skills, use of resources and classroom management. Once they had mastered these they moved on, so the opportunity for discussion and awareness-raising on curriculum development and new methodology was very limited, to everyone's disadvantage.

There are several negative aspects to working with this head of department. She is now very defensive about her work and very demotivated, but she does need to keep her job and realises that without bringing her skills up to date she is unlikely either to be happy in her current position or to be supported in applying for other posts. She is therefore prepared to work to improve her skills but is doing it unwillingly. The case is currently at this stage.

From the head's point of view, he would like to be able to recruit a new head of department but he knows that he is unlikely to appoint anyone potentially better than the present person. Time and money are probably better spent on supporting her to reach a satisfactory standard than in taking the formal route to dismissal for lack of capability. He feels that the scars caused by the OFSTED report will take a long time to heal, that a new start would be better but is not likely to happen and, however unwilling the head of department may be, she is not actually incapable of improving her performance to a satisfactory level. Could the situation have been managed differently? The head could have chosen to deal first with the performance of the head of department, assuming a top-down approach to managing improvement whereby a new head of department would take responsibility for improving teaching, and therefore the work of the teacher, in the department.

A temporary problem

Jane, a year co-ordinator in a primary school

This case explores what can happen when an established member of staff takes over leadership of an existing team. Both the leader and the team have experience of success so do not expect to make adjustments to their working styles. There are lessons to learn here about managing people. When the new teams were created there should have been some discussion in senior management about the dynamics of the new groups and a realisation that Jane was actually changing jobs, even though her title and the job description were the same. Jane's poor performance was not the result of lack of capability, nor of lack of the skills needed to do the job, but of lack of awareness of potential problems.

Jane had been co-ordinator of year 7 in a middle school for seven years when the LEA implemented its plan to change the age of transfer in line with the new Key Stages. Her school changed in status from a middle to a junior school, and her year 7 teacher team was dispersed. The number of year co-ordinators required was the same, as the age of transfer from the first school was also changed, and it was agreed that Jane should become co-ordinator of year 6. In this way her valuable skills and knowledge relating to the transfer of pupils to secondary schools would continue to be used. The other three teachers who had been working with year 7 changed roles: one moved into a secondary school as a specialist art teacher, one took advantage of the good opportunity to take early retirement, and the third (the deputy head) moved to a headship. The co-ordinator of year 6 also took early retirement so the headteacher decided to keep the rest of the staff already working with year 6 together under Jane's leadership.

Jane foresaw no problem with this. She knew the year 6 team to have worked together successfully for several years and assumed that she would just work with them as she had with her own successful teaching team. At first everything seemed to be working smoothly. Meetings were trouble-free as everyone seemed to know what was expected of them and there seemed to be no need for discussions. It was not until half term that Jane began to feel uncomfortable. She had been looking at the planning books of her year 6 teachers, and felt that something was not quite right but could not pinpoint what it was. Then it occurred to her: nothing in the books reflected the policies and action she thought had been agreed by the group. She found the books from the previous year and found that everything was being done exactly as it had with the previous co-ordinator. Feeling secure in the knowledge that their work had been perfectly satisfactory in the past, the group had politely ignored Jane's attempts to make changes. They had seen no need either for change or for any confrontation with Jane. They probably assumed that she would eventually adapt to their ways of working.

Jane now had a dilemma: it had not occurred to her that dynamics could be different in two ostensibly similar groups, and she had taken compliance for assent. She had also let a lot of time elapse before realising her error, so it was now going to be difficult to regain control of the situation. She also realised that her own class was experiencing a somewhat different curriculum from the others in the same year; her teaching reflected her experience with year 7 and could be valuable now that year 6 were the senior year, but all Jane could see was that she was failing both as a manager and as a classroom teacher.

For a while she closed in on herself and was really beginning to fail. Fortunately the deputy head realised that something was wrong and, during a planning meeting with Jane, found the opportunity to hear about the problems. After listening sympathetically she persuaded Jane to look critically at the situation. As a manager she had always succeeded in the past, and as a classroom teacher she had always been able to adapt her practice to incorporate good new ideas. The deputy head suggested she leave her anxieties about her work in the classroom aside while she reasserted herself as leader of the group of teachers working with year 6. To do this, the deputy advised leaving the implementation of the schemes of work for the moment and to look instead at inter-phase liaison and the work that would have to be done to ensure a smooth transition into secondary school. This was the area in which Jane had a lot of successful experience and which was new to the rest of the group. In this way, Jane would be able to take the lead with confidence and induct the others into the new skills required. She would then have re-established her position and would be able to return to the other areas at a later stage.

The head and deputy knew Jane was both a good teacher and a good manager. They agreed that it was worth a delay in implementing some of the targets they had set while Jane recovered her position and her confidence. Furthermore, the school had suffered considerable disruption and lowering of morale during the massive changes wrought by the change in age of transfer, and they knew staff, governors and parents would respond more positively to a slowing down of change implementation than to another period of turbulence as would be caused by a 'hard' response to Jane's temporary poor performance.

A mismatch of personality and school culture

Marcus

Skills, experience and relevant qualifications do not always prove successful when personality and school culture do not match.

Marcus had been an army apprentice. He had joined up at 18 years old with two low grade 'A' levels and had been supported by the army while studying for an HNC in electronics. He had worked in signals for the rest of his commission and came out of the army in 1995, aged 38. Knowing that he would need to prepare for a second career, he had kept up to date with developments in the civilian electronics industry and had involved himself in training and development in his area. In that way he hoped to find work in a company requiring expert trainers. Unfortunately, after six months he found that no opportunities were opening up and he was beginning to be concerned about his financial situation, so he thought again about the training side of his expertise and decided to become a teacher. He took a PGCE as a technology teacher, with ICT as his main area of expertise. He did his teaching practice in a boys grammar school and, although he was not an 'A' grade student, no one voiced any concerns about his potential as a teacher. At first he had trouble finding a teaching job: he had decided that his experience and age qualified him to expect to be appointed at a high point on the salary scale. Heads and governors, however, held the view that he would need the same costly induction programme as any other NQT and that he did not actually offer anything extra that could merit a higher salary. After several interviews where it became clear that he was handicapping himself by this demand, he took advice and agreed to aim at a more reasonable starting salary. He was eventually offered a post in a large comprehensive in the Midlands.

His first few weeks were a disaster. The pupils reacted with hostility to his teaching style, which was very much a reflection of his army experience. Some were frightened of him, some responded by being confrontational; all were unhappy during their lessons with him and eventually complained to the head of department. The head of department's reaction was to pacify them by saying that all new teachers had to set their standards of behaviour from the very first moment, and that as soon as Marcus was sure that they understood his expectations he would relax a little. He then took the opportunity to do what he ought to have been doing from the start, which was to observe Marcus's lessons. (He had assumed that the other, young, NQTs in the department of twelve needed closer observation and had neglected Marcus.) What he found was that there was definitely a problem with Marcus's style, but explaining it and changing it were going to be difficult: it was like a caricature. For example, it was department policy that classes should line up outside the workshops or computer rooms until the teacher allowed them in. Marcus insisted in military precision before letting pupils in. During the lesson, questions were only allowed at designated pauses and all pupils had to work at the same speed, following Marcus's instructions. There was no flexibility, no allowance for investigation, prior knowledge or lack of understanding. This was not teaching and learning, but intensive skills training.

The head of department, Jim, now understood why the pupils felt as they did. Relationships between staff and pupils in the school were generally respectful but friendly (too friendly, according to some of the older staff!) and serious breaches of discipline were rare. Jim spent a lot of time working with Marcus to help him establish a less rigid working style with the pupils. Marcus felt confused because the aspects of his work that were causing the most difficulty had not seemed to cause any problem in the grammar school in which he had done his teaching practice. He was ill at ease with a more relaxed style, and could not accept interaction between himself and the pupils.

Gradually it became clear that Marcus was not able to use a variety of teaching methods, and that he was becoming more and more angry with pupils who did not respond to his methods. Jim was also beginning to lose patience as Marcus's manner was beginning to have an adverse effect on the learning atmosphere in the department and the pupils' progress was being hampered. To make sure that the problem was with Marcus's style and not just a personality difficulty, Jim asked a deputy head to observe some of Marcus's lessons. Her observations reinforced Jim's views, so she suggested that Marcus be allocated some staff development funding to attend a course for teachers of ICT and technology. On his return he agreed that there were other ways of teaching his subject but, even though he tried, he found himself incapable of changing his way of working with the pupils. Since he felt he had been more successful in the boys grammar school, he decided to apply for posts in selective schools. This caused a problem for the head when writing a suitable reference, which was reflected in Marcus's failure to obtain such a post. He did, however, succeed in obtaining a post in an independent school and moved to this at the end of the year.

The increasing tendency to appoint staff on short-term contracts would have been helpful here. It was by no means certain that Marcus would find another post, and the head was torn between the need for honesty on his behalf when writing a reference for an unsuccessful member of staff and the problems that he would be facing if working through the capability procedures. There are still a good many headteachers who do not seem to have such high principles when it is a question of putting their pupils first and of helping an unsatisfactory member of staff move on. It is also difficult to decide whether or not the poor performance in this particular post is because of the culture of the particular school and whether or not the teacher would perform satisfactorily in a different environment. In Marcus's case, he seemed to have worked successfully during his PGCE in a boys grammar school. Maybe the culture there would have been more sympathetic to his teaching style, and the head would have been quite justified in tailoring his reference to suit that environment without voicing the doubts he had about Marcus's qualities as a teacher. There is a very fine balance between being fair to a member of staff and being fair to the receiving establishment, especially when the culture of the latter is not known to the headteacher writing the reference.

Unresolved problems

Steve

This unresolved case explores several issues, not least the effect of a predecessor on the success of a new appointment. It also exemplifies the shortcomings of our traditional recruitment and selection procedures: success in one role in one school cannot be a perfect predictor of success in another situation.

Steve had taken over as teacher in charge of art on the retirement of an eccentric artist who had been running the department his way for longer than anyone in the school could remember. Examination results had always been satisfactory but not outstanding, for Ralph's real skill had been in creating wonderful stage sets for the excellent productions the school was famous for in the town. In his previous job, Steve had quietly established himself as an excellent teacher, able to coax the best out of most of his pupils gently, and proud of the exhibitions he mounted in school and at the local library. It seemed natural, therefore, that he should progress to running his own department.

He moved house in mid-August, giving himself a week to do his share of settling the family into their new house and then a week to make the art rooms his own before term started. This turned out to be a serious underestimation: Ralph had left behind the accumulated material, bric-a-brac and exhibition pieces of twenty years, all kept because 'it could come in useful sometime'. Steve too was not one to throw away anything of potential value, and was by nature painstaking and conscientious. In spite of working every spare minute, he reached the first day of term with very little to show for his hard work, rooms in chaos, planning incomplete and tired out.

This bad start seemed to affect Steve very deeply and he felt that he had got off on the wrong foot altogether. Because he had not succeeded in arranging his rooms how he wanted them, he felt that he had not managed to create the atmosphere he sought for his classes. Because his planning had been done in a great hurry at the last minute, he felt insecure and unable to lead his department (two part-timers) as he would have wished.

He had also not realised that discipline in the department would depend on his lead. He was gentle by nature, best at working with small groups, relying on his ability to motivate the individual rather than managing the behaviour of a full-sized class. In his previous post, his head of department had created by the strength of his own personality an environment that suited Steve's working style. Now it was Steve who was expected to set the standards in the department.

Soon Steve began to feel exhausted. He seemed to be running as fast as he could to keep up with the demands of his new job, but he could not manage to deal simultaneously with staff needing information, pupils needing firm handling and the continuing work on the backlog of organising the physical and material resources for which he was responsible: he still had not worked out how to budget for the department's needs over the coming year.

Not long before Christmas he became ill with the flu. He was ill for most of the holiday and missed the beginning of the new term. This was beginning to become a vicious circle as he was now constantly behind. Try as he might he could not overcome the feeling of exhaustion and some despair that there could be any way out of this situation. He soon found he was missing at least a day a week and felt guilty, angry and helpless. He went to see his doctor, who immediately diagnosed depression and agreed to him staying off work for a month.

Steve wanted to succeed in his job. He had evidence in his previous post that he was a talented teacher, but the combination of so many potential problems made his situation one in which it was impossible to succeed.

From the point of view of the head and governors of the school, they had a failing teacher to deal with. There was no doubt that as things stood Steve was not capable of doing his job, and there was plenty of evidence available to substantiate this if they decided to take the route of formal capability procedures. But would this be the best way forward? Weighing up the situation produces a balance of arguments for and against, as follows:

For:	Against:
Continued absence	Evidence that teacher capable of good work
Difficulties of classroom management	School should take responsibility a for recognising that some of the problems were caused historically and b that they had appointed the teacher
Pupils' impeded progress	Time required to replace current teacher
Lack of staff leadership	Time required to induct new leader

The head and governors, depending on their style and the culture of the school, could therefore argue equally strongly in favour either of following formal capability procedures, which might lead to dismissal and replacement of Steve, or of accepting that they are at least partly responsible for Steve's predicament and for looking at ways to alleviate some of the problems. The first route would probably still take at least two terms — longer before a replacement could be in place and functioning effectively — and could well have a bad effect on relationships within the school. Steve was seen to be trying desperately hard to succeed, so staff sympathies would be with him, even though they knew he was having a lot of difficulties. The second route would also take time and would have no guarantee of success, but would show that poor performance was not tolerated and that staff were supported and given every possible help in overcoming problems. In the long term, this policy would probably have indirect but wider success. Both routes would be costly in terms of both time and material and human resources.

The next problem is to see how Steve's difficulties could be alleviated:

- *first of all he needs to be convinced that the problems are not all of his making, and that practical help could be provided;*
- *then this must be compensated for by completing the organisation of the studios under Steve's direction;*
- *finally, an experienced head of art could be asked to help complete the planning for the current year and work with Steve at a later stage to create the necessary planning documentation.*

The difficulties of classroom management could be helped by some restructuring. Steve was working in some isolation as the head of a very small department, as were the heads of music, drama and dance. If it were possible to group these together under a head of faculty, it could give Steve the type of support he had been used to in his previous post. It would also release him from responsibility for some of the forward planning and attendance at some meetings, thus freeing him up slightly to concentrate on establishing his presence in the classroom. Of course, all this is dependant on there being someone available and suitable to take on the role of head of faculty and the structure being compatible with that elsewhere in the school. In the capability procedures, consideration has to be given to the possibility of the teacher taking on a different role or responsibilities, and it is also possible to deem the teacher lacking in capability as regards their management function but not in their function as a teacher. Steve could be asked to consider stepping down from his head of department role. This is unlikely to be an effective alternative for a teacher developing his career and would probably serve only to demotivate, but is a further possibility if attempts to improve Steve's performance in his present role are not successful.

If this route is followed and all meetings, support given and outcomes are monitored and kept in writing, in the worst-case scenario the capability route is still an option at any stage.

Head of department within a large faculty

The different priorities of different managers within a large, hierarchical institution can lead to different perceptions of both poor performance and ways of dealing with it. At the time of writing, this case is unresolved.

Neil has been head of the science faculty for two years in a very large, high-achieving mixed comprehensive school in a very middle-class area. The school is administered and managed through a structure of six large faculties. Most of the faculty heads are fairly recent appointments and expect to move on to senior teacher or deputy headships. The head of faculty is also in charge of a subject within the faculty, so he has a combined leadership and management role, being the subject expert for part of his role but overseeing the work of other experts leading the other departments. One of the departments under his management is not functioning very well. Last year's GCSE A–C rate in the school was overall 63 per cent; the head of faculty's own subject rate was 78 per cent but the biology department only achieved 48 per cent.

In Neil's view, this poor performance is a reflection of the poor management skills of the head of department. His view is reinforced by value-added data which provide plenty of evidence of the gap widening between biology and other subjects as pupils' performance improves in the other areas.

The biology department has five members of staff. The head of department is 53 years old and has been in post for at least ten years. When Neil took over as head of faculty, the biology department included a newly qualified teacher and a new member of staff, a part-timer working four days a week and a full-timer who was not seen to be a particularly strong teacher. The department seemed to have had a big turnover of staff, with new and young teachers moving on quite quickly. The head of department was mentor to the NQT and to ITT students coming into the department.

Neil saw her to be an 'old style' head of department who believed her role to be mainly ordering stationery and allocating materials. The rest of the teachers in the department seemed to accept this and to a large extent worked as individuals.

Biology is set against history where there is a 'free' option. There are large numbers of pupils opting for biology because pupils see it as easy compared with history and, according to Neil, know it to be made less demanding. Predicted grades are generally in line with actual grades, even though these seem low compared with other subjects, so the head of department seems to be satisfied that the teaching is up to standard. Consistently high numbers of pupils opting for biology further reinforce her view that the department is successful. Neil feels that the results are a self-fulfilling prophecy due to a lack of demanding standards.

The head of biology's own classroom teaching is generally satisfactory. She uses a mixture of methodologies, but Neil feels that she does not seem able to come to grips with differentiation and certainly does not have the skills required to teach new teachers new skills. She does not seem to understand current techniques for assessing learning or for developmental marking of homework.

She is very caring, believing that a 'happy team is a good team', makes no demands on other teachers in her department and does not seem to be able or willing to delegate. Nor does she pass on information or circulate documentation, much to Neil's frustration. She does not convene any formal department meetings, insisting that the team holds its meetings at break, when no developmental work or discussion can take place.

Neil now runs regular faculty meetings in order to create a forum for development for the rest of the biology team, thus taking responsibility away from the head of department. He feels that the whole faculty is not seen to be making progress because this one department lets them down. The previous head of faculty made no demands on the head of biology, being satisfied to allow departments to run autonomously as they had previously. In contrast, the chemistry department is very well-organised and has a new head of department who is keen to develop.

An added frustration for Neil is that the head of biology constantly over-spends capitation, especially on photocopying, being unwilling to plan her spending or to take responsibility for resources. She says that she is doing what is necessary for her teaching.

Neil's impression from discussions with her is that she sees herself as a good and popular teacher. The report after an OFSTED inspection rated biology lessons as predominantly successful (75 per cent satisfactory or good), though there was criticism of the choice of textbook and comment that some lessons were insufficiently challenging. The head of biology does not see management as proactive or that she has a responsibility for the quality of pupils' experience in all biology lessons, not just her own. She sees herself as responding to directives and getting on with her job of teaching to the best of her ability. Neil feels utterly frustrated at being unable to get her to see what else needs doing and that her performance is poor in comparison with that of the rest of the faculty.

When he had been in post for a year, Neil discussed the problem with the senior teacher responsible for staff development. This resulted in a meeting in October with the head of biology and the staff development tutor. Between them they set targets that Neil felt were inadequate, but the head of department said she felt he was being unreasonable in his demands and could only find fault with her. She said he needed to praise her work more rather than constantly putting her down. Neil was by now also becoming concerned about the extent to which this was becoming a personality clash and the difficulty of separating genuine evidence of poor performance from increasing frustration with the person. After all, he was trying to make his mark in the school, like the other ambitious young heads of faculty, and was finding his own progress hampered by what he perceived to be an unwillingness on the part of a colleague to work to his expectations.

To help ease the situation, the head tried to move the head of biology out of her present role and to change her responsibilities – for example, to take responsibility for examinations – but she did not want to change, especially as she seemed to feel she was doing a good job in her current post. She reinforced this during INSET by choosing workshops on pastoral issues (such as drugs), and similarly joining working groups on pastoral issues, even though Neil asked her to join INSET on the role of a head of department. She told him that she felt that she already knew her role, but Neil's view was that she did not want to lose face as an experienced head of department by joining a group seemingly to learn how to do her job!

When the TTA issued material for the proposed qualification for subject leaders, Neil used this as the basis for a checklist for departments under his leadership, working with the other managers in his faculty to measure their current competences and to develop targets. It was soon clear that the head of biology did not match up very well against these targets. But does this constitute grounds for asking the headteacher to consider embarking on capability procedures? Or are they only the results of an ambitious head of faculty experiencing extreme frustration at being unable to move his faculty forward as fast as he would like? Maybe, in his enthusiasm, Neil has tried to implement changes too quickly, not recognising colleagues' different skills, motivation and ability to assimilate new ideas.

The current situation is one of deadlock. The head of faculty is utterly frustrated, and the head of department seems to feel undervalued and persecuted. There is a clear need for someone outside the curriculum area to analyse the problem and help unblock the movement towards improvement. Would the situation be different if senior management had worked more closely with the head of faculty immediately after his appointment? How else could the head of faculty have approached the problem? Why had the head of department been allowed to develop her own methods of working without being monitored? Does the structure of a large school or college risk encouraging incipient poor performance because staff tend to work in isolated groups, setting their own standards without reference to whole school benchmarks? Exchange of ideas, good practice and expectations across the school is more difficult when groups of staff tend to both work and socialise in faculty areas.

If, at this stage, parental complaints are made about biology teaching by the weakest teacher in the department, how should this situation be handled?

A non-teaching member of staff – escalating demands of the job

Maureen, receptionist

Maureen had been the school receptionist for fifteen years. She loved her job, enjoying the status she felt it gave her and the genuine feeling of being at the centre of everything going on in the school. Unfortunately, the requirements of the job had gradually changed without her realising it. The sheer numbers of telephone calls and visitors on site had escalated, so she was doing her best to complete each contact as quickly as possible in order to deal with the next one. She thought she was doing a good job but, in her haste, she was not meeting the needs of either her school or her callers. A large number of callers were tentative prospective parents, likely to be easily put off by what they perceived to be an inappropriate response; others were less tentative and very assertive in their insistence on particular responses (such as being given immediate interviews with members of staff). These callers would, in the past, have been able to speak directly to the head, but he is rarely immediately available. Maureen began to feel very stressed and isolated, as if she was running the school on her own. She had never had a very gentle touch; now her voice acquired a sharp edge to it as she began to feel less and less able to keep up. Colleagues among the staff, parents and even governors complained that they were having their heads bitten off when they rang in to the school or visited reception.

Maureen knew this could not continue for long, but she was frightened to say anything because she felt herself to be the senior member of the administrative team. She did not want to lose face, nor did she want to lose her job. She had no qualifications and little other experience, and could not see where she could obtain another post. Furthermore, she valued the short hours and long holidays as they gave her the time she needed to spend with the real love of her life: her prize-winning spaniels.

In the meantime, some other changes were being considered. The head was concerned about the school image and had set up a working party to find out how parents and local inhabitants viewed the school. Anxieties about the manner of the receptionist were aired, but there also was a lot of concern about there being no one to answer the telephone at lunchtime and between 3.00 and 5.30 p.m. when a lot of people needed to contact the school. The head wanted to consider the idea of having two receptionists working a two-shift pattern: one from 8.30 a.m. to the end of morning school and the other from the beginning of lunchtime to 5.30 p.m. The receptionists would decide how they shared the ten shifts available: either all mornings and all afternoons or a mixture of both.

Maureen was at first very happy with this idea and wanted to have the morning shifts. The other post was advertised. There were no applicants: no one wanted to be paid so little to work hours which always overlapped with children returning home from school. Maureen refused to consider doing a mixture of shifts – it would not suit her routine with the dogs – and it was also felt that she was afraid of losing status if she were not at reception at the busiest times of the day.

The only other alternative was for the job to become full-time. Maureen had no wish at all to take a full-time job, but decided that it was better than losing her job. This was a bad decision. She tried to fit her routine with her dogs around the new working hours, but found she was constantly returning late in the afternoon and was increasingly irritable with anyone who needed her attention just before she was due to go off duty.

The head lost patience with the situation. He was tired of dealing with problems made worse by Maureen's manner at reception, and felt he had ample evidence of her not performing her duties properly. He ended her contract with a month's notice.

The head was within his rights dismissing Maureen. She had accepted the offer of the full-time job and had proved herself incapable of carrying out the duties of that post. Once she had gone, the opportunity returned for two part-time posts to be created with the flexibility needed to be both attractive to potential applicants and to meet the needs of the school. The summary dismissal did however cause a great deal of unrest; many colleagues felt very angry that, as they saw it, Maureen had been forced to leave. But she had been given several opportunities to move out of what was becoming a very stressful situation and what might eventually have led to dismissal anyway. She had not been able to respond to these opportunities in a way that the school could work with, so ultimately she had to leave. We do not know how the head dealt with Maureen through all of this. Did he have good interpersonal skills that enabled negotiations to take place in an amicable, professional manner? Or was there friction and even hostility? Did this further worsen the atmosphere at reception? Did the head take the only route open to him before problems at reception began to have wider repercussions?

Part IV

Chapter 10

A framework for action

This chapter attempts to summarise the findings of the book and provides three summary flowcharts: one for dealing with poor performance (FC1), one with poor performance due to misconduct (FC2) and one with the poor performance of headteachers (FC3).

Prevention

It is clear to all who have had to deal with cases of entrenched poor performance that prevention is far preferable to remediation. Dealing with poor performance is frequently the very unwelcome result of a series of mistakes which have been made in the past and often by others. This means that a first priority should be to prevent poor performance developing.

We believe that it is the effective operation of the processes of staff management which provides the best preventive measures:

- selection
- induction
- motivation and monitoring
- appraisal
- development

Appropriate selection and induction into a well-specified job are the hall-marks of a promising beginning. Thereafter, the person should be within an organisational structure which ensures that someone has responsibility for managing each and every member of staff. That person is the first line of defence in preventing poor performance in his or her staff. It is a manager's responsibility to ensure that the member of staff clearly understands their responsibilities and the particular priorities of the job. This requires a general overview of the performance of the member of staff, and appropriate early action if there is a problem. Failure to detect poor performance is a failure of management.

Every member of staff needs to know that somebody else cares about them and their work performance. Poor performance is much less likely if a member of staff is motivated and helped to develop and refine existing skills and to acquire new ones. A regular appraisal process provides an opportunity for taking stock of the priorities of the job, performance and development, career development and institutional obstacles to better performance.

Policy on poor performance

Before the first case of poor performance arises, it is important that the governing body of a school adopts a policy on how to deal with poor performance. This should include general guidance on performance standards drawn up by the headteacher and agreed by staff. It should include guidance about what steps should be taken if poor performance is suspected. Such clarity and openness should reassure everyone about what is expected and declare that action will be taken about poor performance no matter at what level it should occur.

The governing body should approve the composition and powers of the following committees required for capability and discipline procedures:

- Governors' Staffing First Committee
- Governors' Appeal Hearing

The policy should make clear that poor performance is based on a failure to perform duties at the specified level. Further, this failure will be determined by evidence and that these standards of performance will be equitable and non-discriminatory between different performers of the same tasks. Finally, poor performance will be tackled supportively but, in the interests of children and young people in the school, poor performance cannot be allowed to continue.

Determination to succeed

We believe that it is essential that poor performance and suspected poor performance are approached with a determination to succeed, and that poor performance should be improved or removed: that is, a resolution that the poor performance, if it is confirmed, will be eradicated. The solution should not be predetermined, as there are many ways in which this may be achieved:

- sufficiently improved performance in an unchanged job
- redesigned job
- change of post
- voluntary departure
- dismissal

The solution should depend upon the causes of poor performance and the particular circumstances. However, we wish to emphasise that at the outset we believe that the manager dealing with a poor performer should resolve that, if performance cannot be raised sufficiently and none of the other solutions is appropriate, then the solution should be dismissal of the poor performer in the interests of the school and its students. We wish to emphasise that we regard this as the least likely possibility if the procedures in this book are followed. We believe such resolution is necessary, however, because we have encountered so many cases where, in the early stages, any improvement in performance was regarded as acceptable. The problem was then regarded as solved, but reappeared when the next complaint was received.

At an early stage, a manager must formulate what should be the features which show sufficient improvement to demonstrate that the school's benchmark for poor performance has been clearly exceeded. These features should be the same as would be accepted as satisfactory for other staff. This must be the fixed target, and any flexibility should be concerned with how this change is accomplished. We are not seeking to press for dismissals, and nothing in the remainder of this book should be taken to signal this, but we do regard this as a possibility if all else fails.

We are only too aware that poor performance is an extremely sensitive issue. We recognise that some will seek to misunderstand and misrepresent our ideas for political purposes or out of self-interest, so we are trying as best we can to prevent this by making as clear as possible the dilemma which may arise between the interests of the poor performer and the interests of the children and young people who are not receiving their entitlement. This is most acute when, despite determined efforts, performance fails to improve sufficiently. There may be no painless solution. We cannot recommend a solution that will suit all circumstances. All we can do is to recommend a process which, if faithfully carried out, will ensure that justice is done for all concerned.

We are anxious to see poor performance remedied and not for poor performers to be dismissed. We have written this book not only to tackle poor performers, but also to try to ensure that these processes are carried out in a fair and supportive way, with the interests of children and young people in schools as the ultimate priority. We believe that this may improve the present position in schools, which is often somewhat inconsistent. Often the rhetoric and espoused theory is that there are no poor performers in individual schools, and, if there were, they would be supported, while the reality or theory-in-use is that any poor performance is dealt with in a most discriminatory and prejudiced manner. We wish to see a supportive but firm approach both espoused and in use.

Dealing with suspected poor performance

Suspected poor performance can be discovered through a variety of means, both proactive and reactive. Following the preventive advice given here, poor performance should be spotted, or at least a problem noticed, by the manager who has an overview of the work of the member of staff in question. This may be as a result of seeing or hearing certain incidents, or a more formal assessment of performance in action, or the outcomes of performance as demonstrated by the learning of pupils when the results of one teaching group are compared with others. A more reactive approach waits for a problem to be brought to the attention of the management of a school: for example, as a consequence of OFSTED school inspections, or complaints from pupils, staff or parents.

The first stage is to investigate and collect evidence. The emphasis should be on evidence. This will allow others to assess the evidence more impartially rather than having to accept whatever conclusion the investigator reaches. Evidence can come from a number of sources and is more convincing when it comes from a number of sources in a number of forms. Both actual performance and the results or outcomes of performance can be investigated.

When evidence has been collected, then this evidence needs weighing up. Not all evidence has equal weight. Specific performance problems may be identified but, for the purposes of this book, an overall judgement is required as to whether the performance of the person is above or below the benchmark of what a satisfactory performer could and should achieve in these circumstances. If the judgement is that there are some aspects of poor performance within a generally satisfactory level of performance, then some remedial targets can be set which should deal with the problem.

Where the problems are more serious, and the general level of performance is unsatisfactory, or key elements are poor, then the more comprehensive procedures appearing in the poor performers flowchart (FC1) should be triggered.

After preliminary evidence suggests that there is a problem of poor performance, an informal interview should be held with the suspected poor performer to talk about the evidence which is giving rise to concerns. This should deal with the evidence and aim to reach agreement on whether or not there is clear evidence of poor performance. If agreement cannot be reached, further evidence may be necessary until the case is overwhelming. Once poor performance is agreed, the investigation moves on to causes and then possible solutions.

Causes of poor performance

This calls for further investigation. The investigation which confirmed poor performance may have suggested possible causes. The line taken in this book is that other possibilities should be considered and eliminated before assuming that the cause lies exclusively with the employee.

The other causes which should be investigated are:

- the way in which the individual is, and has been, managed
- the nature of the job and all its aspects

It may be that the person is, or has been, managed ineffectively or not managed at all. Performance may never have been raised as an issue before.

The alternative possibility is that the job, as currently conceived, is either not feasible, or has elements that are not feasible, for the particular employee. In this case the job may need to be considered for change. This needs to be considered in light of an assessment of the employee and his or her motivation and skills.

Just as there are a number of causes or contributors to poor performance, so there are a number of solutions, and these must be related to an assessment of the prevailing circumstances; or, in other words, be contingent on the evidence, rather than predetermined solutions being enforced. A short range of solutions are covered in the next section.

Dealing with confirmed poor performance

A summary table with five questions used in earlier chapters with summary answers and implications is shown below in Table 10.1.

Table 10.1 Summary questions and implications for dealing with poor performers

	Question	Answer	Implications
1	Do they know what they should be doing?	Yes	Supervision and proceed to question 2
		No	Job description and supervision
2	Can the job be done by a normally competent person?	Yes	Proceed to question 3
		No	Job redesign
3	Do they have the skills to do it?	Yes	Proceed to question 5
		No	Job modification, change of job or training and question 4
4	Could they acquire the skills?	Yes	Training and support
		No	Job modification, change of job or dismissal
5	Could they do it if their job depended on it?	Yes	Motivation, coercion or dismissal
		No	Dismissal

The very first questions must be: does the poor performer know that their performance is unacceptable and do they know the level of performance which is required? If the answer to either of these questions could be yes, then a communication and clarifications exercise is called for. As a result of this, targets can be set which need to be monitored. If the diagnosis is that the person has the skills but has not deployed them, then the setting of targets alone may not be sufficient. The sufficiency may depend upon the willingness of the person to fulfil the requirements of satisfactory performance. If, however, a lack of skill has been identified, then the stages of professional support should be considered.

Thus, the next fundamental decision is concerned with whether the route should be discipline or whether professional support procedures are called for. In part, this decision depends on the nature and seriousness of the poor performance and an assessment of the competence and motivation of the poor performer:

1   If the poor performance is serious and endangers others, discipline should be considered. We judge this to be highly unusual, but there may be a fine line between misconduct and failing to carry out a necessary act that might be viewed as poor performance.
2   If an assessment of the competence of the poor performer suggests that they could perform better and at an acceptable level but are failing to do so wilfully, then discipline should be considered.

Professional advice and guidance

In this book we have provided generalised advice and recommended an approach to dealing with poor performance. However, for all except foundation and aided schools it is the LEA which is the employer of teachers and other staff. The governing body has certain legal rights but, in the main, it is the headteacher operating in the capacity of delegated manager by the employing LEA who is empowered to carry out the early stages of dealing with poor performance. The appropriate procedures for professional support and discipline are those which have been adopted by the employing LEA and so it is important that these are followed. We recognise that the employing LEA is in the best position to provide details of these procedures and give practical advice about how to follow them.

On the flowcharts, we have suggested the appropriate stages when we consider the employing LEA should be consulted for personnel and legal advice. We have assumed that such contact, once made, will be continued and so we have not specifically signalled further LEA advice at each subsequent stage. As we emphasised in Chapter 6, the LEA is one source of advice for the governing body in carrying out its statutory powers, but should not be taken to be the only one if the governing body does not believe that the advice is either correct or in the best interests of the school. In this case it should seek alternative professional advice.

In addition to legal and personnel advice, the LEA may also be the most appropriate source of professional advice about the performance of teachers. An advisor or inspector who has seen many teachers in similar circumstances may be able to provide a valuable comparative perspective on the level of performance, and also to offer advice on possible solutions in cases of confirmed poor performance. Such an assessment has the great advantage of being independent of the school and is thus valuable corroborative evidence where poor performance is not accepted by a poor performer.

Discipline

Formal disciplinary procedures exist to ensure that employees are aware of their errors and to give them the opportunity of putting right any deficiencies in their performance. If they fail to do so, then dismissal can be expected to follow.

In addition to disciplinary procedures, professional support procedures are available for teaching staff but are not generally available to other staff who work in schools. So, for this larger group, disciplinary procedures are all that is available. It should be remembered, therefore, that for non-teaching staff discipline has to cover both lack of competence and lack of will to give adequate performance. Where it is lack of capacity, then similar help should be made available to teaching support staff as is available to teachers under the professional support agreements.

A summary flowchart covering discipline (FC2) follows later, but this should be read in conjunction with the flowchart on poor performance (FC1), since discipline is only considered here as it may arise in the course of dealing with poorly performing staff. The discipline chart (FC2) assumes that some stages of dealing with poor performers have already taken place.

Professional support

Professional support procedures have been agreed with teachers' professional associations and represent an attempt to ensure that those who are not performing adequately receive help and training to improve their performance. However, this assumes that it is lack of skill which is causing poor performance, and that this lack of skill can be remediated by training and other forms of support. Where these conditions are not fulfilled, disciplinary action should be considered instead.

Where the problem is likely to be solved by enhanced skills, then there should be consideration of how these skills are best acquired. Quite likely this can be achieved by a mixture of off-site training and mentoring on-site. Targets for improvement need to be set which are SMART (specific, measurable, agreed, realistic, time-bounded).

Alternative solutions

A range of more inventive solutions to the issue of poor performance has been suggested in Chapter 4, when training and development are not appropriate actions. These include:

- redesigning parts of the job
- changing jobs within a school
- taking a job in another school
- voluntary departure

Finally, a series of three flowcharts provide guidance through the sequence of steps involved in identifying and dealing with poor performance. FC1 deals with poor performance in teaching and non-teaching staff below the level of headteacher. FC2 takes the case where poor performance should be dealt with by disciplinary procedures after it has first been identified. FC3 takes the case of poor performance of headteachers. In this case, and this case alone, it is the governing body who must initiate action by the LEA.

Flowchart FC1: A flowchart for suspected poor performance

The flowchart consists of a series of steps which are conditional on the answers to specified questions. At each question there are two possible answers. Result 1 leads on to the next step while result 2 suggests some other course of action. Although each step is listed separately, it may not require action but is intended to act as a reminder to consider that point.

FC1 Summary flowchart for poor performance

Step	Decision	Result 1	Result 2
1	Is it the head?	No	Yes: Governors' problem – see separate chart (FC3)
2	Is there actually a problem?	Head investigates and gathers evidence	
3		Yes	No: discover reason for false alarm
4	Has the person done something wrong at work?	No	Yes: consider discipline procedure; suspend for gross misconduct or begin disciplinary procedure for misconduct – see separate chart (FC2)
5	Has the person failed to do something which he or she should have done?	Yes	No: for poor performance, continue at step 7
6	Is this wilful failure?	No	Yes: consider disciplinary procedure – see separate chart (FC2)
7		Interview with suspected poor performer	
8	Is a further professional opinion on performance required?	Yes: call LEA advisor or other professional	No: proceed to step 10
9	Does this confirm the problem?	Yes	No: discover reason for false alarm
10	Should the problem have been spotted previously?	Yes	No: no reflection on manager; involve him or her in solving problem – proceed to step 12
11	Is the problem already being monitored by the manager?	No	Yes: discuss with manager how the problem should be progressed – proceed to step 12

12	Is legal advice necessary?	No: proceed to step 13
	There are two problems: (1) poor performer and (2) manager (treat separately from step 10) Yes: call on LEA for legal and personnel advice or other qualified source	
13	Problem (1): How long has there been a problem?	Long-standing problem Temporary problem: investigate causes for changes in person, circumstances or job; identify speedy remediation or proceed to 15
14	Does the person know what he or she should be doing and clearly understand the priorities of the job?	Yes No: clarify job description, help prioritise and set performance standards and monitor
15	Does he or she want to do a satisfactory job?	Yes No: motivation problem – could involve discipline (FC2)
16	Could the person do the job if their job depended on it?	Yes No: dismissal for incapacity
17		Formal interview: agree targets, how performance will be assessed, timescale, support and monitor
18	Is additional training required?	No Yes: ensure training provided and proceed to step 19
19	Sufficient improvement?	Yes No: suspend pending Governors' Staffing First Committee and dismissal
20	Continue to monitor to ensure satisfactory performance is continued	

Flowchart FC2: discipline problem arising from suspected poor performance (FCI steps 4, 6 or 15)

If an initial case of poor performance is diagnosed as requiring disciplinary procedures start at step (a). Each decision has two possible results. If the result is in the first column, proceed to the next step. If the result is in the second column, follow the instructions.

FC2 Flowchart for poor performance involving discipline

Step	Decision	Result 1	Result 2
(a)	Is this misconduct or gross misconduct?	Misconduct	Gross misconduct: suspend pending a hearing which could result in dismissal
(b)	Is the case serious enough to proceed with discipline?	Yes	No: informal warning
(c)	Is an oral warning appropriate?	Yes	No: proceed to appropriate more serious sanction
(d)	Stage 1	Oral warning: copy kept on file for the period laid down by the relevant procedures	
(e)	Has there been a further incident within the prescribed period?	Yes	No: disregard file note
(f)	Stage 2	Written warning: copy kept on file for the period laid down by the relevant procedures	
(g)	Has there been a further incident within the prescribed period?	Yes: proceed to final written warning	No: disregard letter
(h)	Stage 3	Final written warning	
(i)	Has conduct improved sufficiently?	No: proceed to a hearing for dismissal	Yes: disregard final warning after the period laid down by the relevant procedures
(j)	Advise LEA of intention to dismiss		
(k)	Stage 4	Dismissal	

Flowchart FC3: problem with headteacher arising from poor performance (FC1 step 1)

At each step, when there is a question there are two possible results. For result 1 proceed to the next step, while for result 2 follow the appropriate guidance.

FC3 Flowchart for poorly performing headteacher

Step	Decision	Result 1	Result 2
A	What is the nature of any evidence?	Strong: e.g. OFSTED, LEA report or staff or parental complaints	Suspicions only: seek professional advice from LEA or other professional advisor
B		Seek legal and professional advice from LEA or other qualified source	
C		Ask LEA to investigate and report	
D	What is the result of LEA investigation?	Strong evidence of problem	*No evidence:* investigate reason for false alarm *Weak evidence:* Can the governing body continue to work with the headteacher? If no, proceed to E.
E	Is there a realistic chance of improvement through capability procedures?	Yes: ask LEA to institute procedures	No: investigate voluntary departure or dismissal
F	What is the result of LEA procedures?	Improvement: continue to monitor performance until there is assurance of satisfactory performance	No improvement: move to a hearing which could result in dismissal

References and further reading

The list of references below gives details of any sources cited in the text. The suggestions for further reading are in two parts. There is a section which gives further reading associated with each chapter. These are few in number and mainly cover other writing by the authors since they follow the same approach offered here, but each gives many more references to follow up. The other section of further reading gives a number of books, mostly concerned with dealing with poor performance in general work settings rather than schools.

References

Bramson, R M. (1981) *Coping With Difficult People*, New York: Bantam Doubleday Dell.
Brock, P. (1991) 'Small school headships and the dual function. A study of some of the problems which arise as a result of the dual function and of ways in which effective management may be achieved', unpublished MSc dissertation, University of Reading.
DfEE (1997a) *School Governors: A Guide To The Law* (June 1997 edition), London: DfEE.
—— (1997b) *Revised Outline Capability Procedure for Teachers*, London: DfEE.
—— (1998) *Draft Code of Practice on LEA–School Relations*, London: DfEE.
Drummond, H. (1990) *Managing Difficult Staff: Effective Procedures and the Law*, London: Kogan Page.
Fidler, B. (1992) 'Handling Poor Performers', in B. Fidler and R. Cooper (eds), *Staff Appraisal and Staff Management in Schools and Colleges: A Guide to Implementation*, Harlow: Longman.
Fidler, B., Earley, P., Ouston, J. and Davies, J. (1998) 'Teacher Gradings and OFSTED Inspection: Help or Hindrance as a Management Tool?', *School Leadership and Management* 18(2): 257–70.
The Funding Agency for Schools (1999) *Sharing Experiences: Value for Money in School Management*.
Honey, P. (1980) *Solving People-Problems*, Maidenhead: McGraw-Hill.

Latham, G.P., Cummings, L.L. and Mitchell, T.R. (1987) 'Behavioral Strategies to Improve Productivity,' in R.M. Steers and L.W. Porter (eds) *Motivation and Work Behavior*, 4th edn, New York: McGraw-Hill.

Mager, R.F. and Pipe, P. (1990) *Analysing Performance Problems: or You Really Oughta Wanna*, 2nd edn, London: Kogan Page (Class no. 658.3125; Access no. 200549).

Mitchell, T.R. and Green, S.G. (1983) 'Leadership and Poor Performance: An Attributional Analysis', in J.R. Hackman, E.E. Lawler and L.W. Porter (eds), *Perspectives on Behavior in Organizations*, 2nd edn, New York: McGraw-Hill

Morgan, G. (1996) 'Managing the small primary school: the dual role of teacher/manager', unpublished MSc dissertation, University of Reading.

Stewart, V. and Stewart, A. (1982) *Managing the Poor Performer*, Aldershot: Gower Press.

Further reading by chapter

Chapter 2

Beardwell, I. and Holden, L. (1994) *Human Resource Management*, London: Pitman.

Belbin, R.M. (1993) *Team Roles at Work*, Oxford: Butterworth-Heinemann.

Caulkin, S. (1998) 'How That Pat on the Head can mean Money in the Bank', *The Observer* Business Section: Work, 19 April 1998, p. 1.

Fidler, B. (1992) 'How to Get the Top Job', *Times Education Supplement*, 21 February 1992, p. 17.

—— (1997a) 'Organisational Structure and Organisational Effectiveness', in A. Harris, N. Bennett and M. Preedy (eds), *Organisational Effectiveness and Improvement in Education*, Milton Keynes: Open University Press.

—— (1997b) 'Addressing the Tensions: Culture and Values', in B. Fidler, S. Russell and T. Simkins (eds), *Choices for Self-managing Schools: Autonomy and Accountability*, London: Paul Chapman.

Fidler, B. and Cooper, R. (eds) (1992) *Staff Appraisal and Staff Management in Schools and Colleges: A Guide to Implementation*, Harlow: Longman.

Fidler, B., Bowles, G. and Hart, J. (1991) *ELMS Workbook: Planning Your School's Strategy*, Harlow: Longman.

Tomlinson, H. (ed.) (1997) *Managing Continuing Professional Development*, London: Paul Chapman.

Chapter 3

Beckett, J.T. (1982) 'Assessment of Departmental Performance in Examinations', *Educational Management and Administration* 10(3): 233–6.

Bramson, R.M. (1981) *Coping With Difficult People*, New York: Bantam Doubleday Dell.

DfEE (1997b) *Revised Outline Capability Procedure for Teachers*, London: DfEE.

Everard, K.B. and Morris, G. (1996) *Effective School Management*, 3rd edn, London: Paul Chapman.

Francis, D. (1990) *Effective Problem Solving*, London: Routledge.

Willms, J.D. (1992)*Monitoring School Performance: A Guide for Educators*, Lewes: Falmer Press.

Chapter 4

Bramson, R.M. (1981) *Coping With Difficult People*, New York: Bantam Doubleday Dell.
Everard, K.B. and Morris, G. (1996) *Effective School Management*, 3rd edn, London: Paul Chapman.
Fidler, B. (1997) 'The School as a Whole: School Improvement and Planned Change', in B. Fidler, S. Russell and T. Simkins (eds), *Choices for Self-managing Schools: Autonomy and Accountability*, London: Paul Chapman.

Chapter 5

DfEE (1997) *Revised Outline Capability Procedure for Teachers*, London: DfEE
—— (1997) *School Governors: A Guide to the Law* (June 1997 edition), London: DfEE.
—— (1998) *Draft Code of Practice on LEA–School Relations*, London: DfEE.

Chapter 6

DfEE (1997) *Revised Outline Capability Procedure for Teachers*, London: DfEE.
—— (1997) *School Governors: A Guide to the Law* (June 1997 edition), London: DfEE.
Fidler, B., Earley, P., Ouston, J. and Davies, J. (1998) 'Teacher Gradings and OFSTED Inspection: Help or Hindrance as a Management Tool?', *School Leadership and Management* 18(2): 257–70.

Chapter 7

DfEE (1998) *Draft Code of Practice on LEA–School Relations*, London: DfEE.
Fidler, B. (1997) 'The Case for School Leadership', in K. Watson, C. Modgil and S. Modgil (eds), *Educational Dilemmas: Debate and Diversity*, vol. 3: *Power and Responsibility in Education*, London: Cassell.
TTA (1997) *The National Professional Qualification for Headship: Candidates' Pack*, London: TTA.

Further books on poor performers in general work settings

Bramson, R.M. (1981) *Coping With Difficult People*, New York: Bantam Doubleday Dell.
Brinkman, R. and Kirschner, R. (1994) *Dealing With People You Can't Stand*, New York: McGraw-Hill.

Bruce, W.M. (1990) *Problem Employee Management: Proactive Strategies for Human Resource Managers*, Westport, CT: Quorum Books.

Cava, R. (1990) *Dealing with Difficult People: Proven Strategies for Handling Stressful Situations and Defusing Tensions*, New York: Piatkus Books.

de la Bedoyere, Q. (1989) *Managing People and Problems*, Aldershot: Wildwood House.

Drummond, H. (1990) *Managing Difficult Staff: Effective Procedures and the Law*, London: Kogan Page.

Gallagher, T.J. (1987) *Problem Solving with People*, Lanham, MD: University Press of America.

Honey, P. (1980) *Solving People-Problems*, Maidenhead: McGraw-Hill.

—— (1992) *Problem People and How to Manage Them*, London: IPM.

Mager, R.F. and Pipe, P. (1990) *Analysing Performance Problems: or You Really Oughta Wanna*, 2nd edn, London: Kogan Page (Class no. 658.3125; Access no. 200549).

Steinmetz, L.L. (1985) *Managing the Marginal and Unsatisfactory Performer*, 2nd edn, Reading, MA: Addison Wesley (Class no. 658.3; Access no. 200288).

Stewart, V. and Stewart, A. (1982) *Managing the Poor Performer*, Aldershot: Gower Press.

Wheeler, M. (1994) *Problem People at Work and How to Deal with Them*, London: Century Business.

Wylie, P. and Grothe, M. (1991) *Problem Employees: How to Improve Their Behaviour and Their Performance*, London: Piatkus.

Further short booklets on poorly performing teachers in schools

Barker, B. (1996) *Back Me or Sack Me: Strategies for Managing Low and Poor Performance in Schools*, London: Industrial Society.

Trethowan, D. (1991) *Improving the Unsatisfactory Teacher Performance*, London: Industrial Society. This is a 30-page pamphlet of advice.

A book emphasising the legal aspects of staff management

Potter, E. and Smellie, D. (1995) *Managing staff problems fairly: A guide for schools*, Kingston Upon Thames: Croner.

Index